SYLVIA PLATH

Recent Titles in Greenwood Biographies

Billy Graham: A Biography
Roger Bruns

Emily Dickinson: A Biography
Connie Ann Kirk

Langston Hughes: A Biography
Laurie F. Leach

Fidel Castro: A Biography
Thomas M. Leonard

Oprah Winfrey: A Biography
Helen S. Garson

Mark Twain: A Biography
Connie Ann Kirk

Jack Kerouac: A Biography
Michael J. Dittman

Mother Teresa: A Biography
Meg Greene

Jane Addams: A Biography
Robin K. Berson

Rachel Carson: A Biography
Arlene R. Quaratiello

Desmond Tutu: A Biography
Steven D. Gish

Marie Curie: A Biography
Marilyn Bailey Ogilvie

Ralph Nader: A Biography
Patricia Cronin Marcello

Carl Sagan: A Biography
Ray Spangenburg and Kit Moser

SYLVIA PLATH

A Biography

Connie Ann Kirk

GREENWOOD BIOGRAPHIES

GREENWOOD PRESS
WESTPORT, CONNECTICUT · LONDON

Library of Congress Cataloging-in-Publication Data

Kirk, Connie Ann.
    Sylvia Plath : a biography / Connie Ann Kirk.
       p. cm.—(Greenwood biographies, ISSN 1540–4900)
    Includes bibliographical references and index.
    ISBN 0–313–33214–2
    1. Plath, Sylvia. 2. Poets, American—20th century—Biography. 3. Hughes, Ted,
1930—Marriage. I. Title. II. Series.
PS3566.L27Z747   2004
811'.54—dc 22   2004018482

British Library Cataloguing in Publication Data is available.

Library of Congress Catalog Card Number: 2004018482
ISBN: 0–313–33214–2
ISSN: 1540–4900

First published in 2004

Greenwood Press, 88 Post Road West, Westport, CT 06881
An imprint of Greenwood Publishing Group, Inc.
www.greenwood.com

Printed in the United States of America

The paper used in this book complies with the
Permanent Paper Standard issued by the National
Information Standards Organization (Z39.48–1984).

10 9 8 7 6 5 4 3 2 1

to Ken

CONTENTS

Series Foreword   ix

Preface   xi

Timeline   xv

Chapter 1 Who Was Sylvia? Beyond the Icon   1

Chapter 2 Early Life and Family (pre-1932–1936)   7

Chapter 3 The Golden Schoolgirl (1937–1955)   17

Chapter 4 The Academic Life (1950–1955)   35

Chapter 5 A Poet's Life and a Poet's Wife (1956–1961)   67

Chapter 6 The Bell Jar Cracks (1962–1963)   89

Chapter 7 After Plath: Mysteries and Controversies   105

Appendix A: Family Tree   113

Appendix B: Sylvia Plath's Library   115

Bibliography   121

Index   129

Photo essay follows page 66

SERIES FOREWORD

In response to high school and public library needs, Greenwood developed this distinguished series of full-length biographies specifically for student use. Prepared by field experts and professionals, these engaging biographies are tailored for high school students who need challenging yet accessible biographies. Ideal for secondary school assignments, the length, format and subject areas are designed to meet educators' requirements and students' interests.

Greenwood offers an extensive selection of biographies spanning all curriculum related subject areas including social studies, the sciences, literature and the arts, history and politics, as well as popular culture, covering public figures and famous personalities from all time periods and backgrounds, both historic and contemporary, who have made an impact on American and/or world culture. Greenwood biographies were chosen based on comprehensive feedback from librarians and educators. Consideration was given to both curriculum relevance and inherent interest. The result is an intriguing mix of the well known and the unexpected, the saints and sinners from long-ago history and contemporary pop culture. Readers will find a wide array of subject choices from fascinating crime figures like Al Capone to inspiring pioneers like Margaret Mead, from the greatest minds of our time like Stephen Hawking to the most amazing success stories of our day like J. K. Rowling.

While the emphasis is on fact, not glorification, the books are meant to be fun to read. Each volume provides in-depth information about the subject's life from birth through childhood, the teen years, and adulthood. A thorough account relates family background and education, traces personal and professional influences, and explores struggles, accomplishments, and contributions. A timeline highlights the most significant life events against a historical perspective. Bibliographies supplement the reference value of each volume.

PREFACE

As most authors have probably experienced at one time or another, sometimes a confluence of events and odd coincidences seem to gather and swirl over a book in progress until the author begins to feel like a vehicle for some unknown force pushing the book into being. The day I signed the contract to write *Sylvia Plath: A Biography* for Greenwood Press, the fourth title I've written for the Greenwood Biographies series, was the same day the film *Sylvia*, starring Gwyneth Paltrow, came to a cinema in my area. As I sat in the theater on that Saturday evening, November 7, 2003, a full, bright, and completely visible lunar eclipse occurred over the Northeast from 8:07 until 8:31 P.M., directly visible over the cinema, I was told later, during the dead center of the film as I watched it. Those familiar with Plath's work, with its loaded and frequent imagery of the moon, will fully understand why the intersection of these three events on a single day struck me as a bit serendipitous, to say the least.

The strange coincidences continued as I researched the book. Rereading Plath's journals through that following winter, I caught myself turning up the thermostat during several deep freezes in one of the coldest winters the Northeast has had in a few years. As the reader will learn, Plath died during one of the coldest winters in England's history. Later, my research took me to Smith College in Northampton, Massachusetts, where Plath spent time both as a student and an instructor. The first day I happened to be there, though I did not recall it until a short time afterwards, marked the 48th anniversary of Sylvia Plath's first meeting with Ted Hughes.

These odd coincidences and others shed years away from the time in graduate school when I, like so many other young, female American writers, went through my "Plath period" and survived. What is a "Plath period?" To this writer, it is the time when Sylvia Plath's internal struggle over competing desires for perfection in art and family life become dramatized in one's own life (often over-dramatized by sensitive young women, who because of their age and temperament, think their lives at that moment are the only ones worth considering). Though that period in a young writer's life may last a few days or several months, reading Plath's concerns makes them become intensely familiar and understood. To young college students of English or art or music, the frustrations Plath expresses in her journals of living as a female and an artist in Western society strike a painful and recognizable chord.

Not every person who goes through long nights of youthful angst worrying about one's future devotion to art and job and/or family contemplates suicide as an alternative, but many are drawn to the edge that Plath leaped off, if only to peer at the drama of it out of curiosity. Thankfully, most of us are healthy enough to be able to pull back and move on toward futures of life and work and love that involve caring for other people and they for us. Unfortunately, like so many artists who have ended their own lives, Sylvia Plath has engendered a cult following of those who cannot seem to pull themselves back from that edge and instead linger there or are unable to leave due to their own neuroses, illnesses, or for other reasons, toying with dangerous and unhealthy thoughts. To any of these young people who may have picked up this book to read about Sylvia Plath, woman and poet, as mythical icon or artist martyr, I would like to say up front—hold on.

While it is true that the darkness of the poet's suicide casts a cool, ever-present shadow over her work and life, and any biography must describe and come to terms with that, this book takes the approach that a human being and an artist is more than a carrier and victim of whatever illness it was that killed him/her. If Artist X dies from cancer, which she fought for many years, that fact contributes to, but does not define, her life. Mental illness should be treated no differently.

Plath is one of the most anthologized and problematic American poets of the twentieth century. Not unlike the nineteenth-century poet Emily Dickinson, whose biography I also wrote for this series, stories about Plath's life and death have been plagued by controversies that make presenting an accurate account particularly difficult for the biographer. In writing this book, my intent has been, as it was with Dickinson, to try to peel away some of the mysteries that have accumulated over the years and cast the poet's life in a more balanced, realistic light. While the poet remains a cult figure for many, she was a real woman who experienced contentment in her life and struggled with the smaller everyday cares and concerns that all of us do, and not just with the dramatic issues of mental breakdowns or passionate romances for which she is most known.

Most of all, Sylvia Plath was a female artist working within the confines of her time in the post–World War II era of the 1950s and 1960s. Her short life experience has much to tell us about women writers of the period that is worth examining for its cultural insights. Unlike the scanty records available on Emily Dickinson, Plath left behind in her journals, calendars, papers, and manuscripts a plethora of material for any biographer to pore over and contemplate. In addition, Plath was a comparatively public figure in a time when public records such as school attendance and awards were also kept, so there are newspaper articles and other kinds of public documents available as resource material. Finally, since Plath is a figure who has been gone only four decades, family members and contemporaries who knew her are still around to offer reminiscences and written memoirs.

My working methods included consulting the most respected full-length biographies as well as guardedly reading those with obvious biases; reading personal memoirs of those who knew Plath and interviewing one contemporary who knew her; researching her correspondence; and listening to and viewing audio and video recordings of the poet reading and being interviewed about her work. In addition, I also researched the world's two most extensive Plath archives—at the Lilly Library at Indiana University as well as the vast holdings at Smith College.

My work was advanced significantly by receiving an Everett Helm Research Fellowship from the Lilly Library to study the Plath archives. There I was able to examine the poet's childhood diaries and journals; her baby book and other mementoes kept by her mother; her books, including her heavily annotated *Portable James Joyce*; unpublished photographs; her calendars, including the fateful year of 1953; her high school yearbook and scrapbook; several works of original art and many other papers, letters, and memorabilia. At Smith, I was able to examine such pertinent materials as her famous published journals in their raw, handwritten form; books from her library with handwritten markings and annotations; personal calendars, including 1962–1963; original drawings and sketches; handwritten and early typescript manuscripts for poems, including those of her final collection, *Ariel*, as well as the novel *The Bell Jar*; and a last letter she wrote to friends days before her death in which she looks forward to spring. This biography has been informed by all of the above important primary materials and more.

My thanks go to Lynn Araujo of Greenwood for inviting me to write the book. I also thank the Helm Fellowship committee of Indiana University; Breon Mitchell, Director of the Lilly Library; and also the excellent staff at that facility for the generosity of the fellowship and their assistance as I examined the Plath archives. Thanks also go to Karen V. Kukil, Associate Curator of Rare Books at the Mortimer Rare Book Room at Smith College's William Allan Neilson Library, for her gracious and generous help with Plath's manuscripts, papers, and other archival materials. Ms. Kukil is the editor of *The Unabridged Journals of Sylvia Plath*, so her particular knowledge of the Smith collection and the journals, as well as her insights into Plath's life and sensibilities and her recommendations of secondary sources, were invaluable to this project. Thanks also go to Polly Longsworth for her personal reminiscences and insights into Plath's presence as a classmate at Smith.

My fabulous five—Ken, my husband of over 20 years; wonderful sons Ben and John; and my dear parents, Len and Mary Lewis, married 60 years—sustain me with their love and devotion in ways beyond measure. They have helped prove in my own life that it is not only possible for art and family life to coexist, but it is also possible for them to nurture one another for the benefit of both. I wish Sylvia Plath had lived long enough to experience that gift.

TIMELINE

(Note: Historical and cultural events are marked in bold.)

13 April 1885	Otto Emil Platt (Plath), the poet's father, is born at Grabow, Germany, the first of six children of blacksmith, Theodore, and homemaker, Ernestine (Kottke) Platt.
15 May 1886	**Poet Emily Dickinson dies in Amherst, Massachusetts.**
1900	Otto Platt emigrates to the United States, changing his surname to Plath. Settles in New York City with his uncle, clerking in his store and auditing English classes.
1902	Franz (Frank) Schober, the poet's maternal grandfather, emigrates to the United States from Austria, via Paris and London.
1903	Otto Plath moves from New York City to Watertown, Wisconsin, to attend prep school, promising his grandparents, who are underwriting his education, that he will enter the seminary to become a Lutheran minister.
1904	Aurelia Grunwald (Greenwood), the poet's maternal grandmother, emigrates to the United States from Austria.
10 July 1905	Frank Schober and Aurelia Greenwood, the poet's maternal grandparents, are married in Boston, Massachusetts.

26 April 1906	Aurelia Frances Schober, the poet's mother, is born in Massachusetts.
Fall 1906	Otto Plath enters Northwestern College, Watertown, Wisconsin, majoring in classical languages. Acquires interest in biology after reading Darwin. While at Northwestern, marries Lydia Bartz, but separates months later.
1910	Otto Plath graduates from Northwestern and enters Wisconsin Lutheran Seminary in Wauwatosa. Drops out weeks later and is disowned by his grandfather, John, who crosses Otto's name out of the Plath family Bible. Plath teaches and studies German in Seattle.
1912	Otto Plath earns M. A., German, University of Washington. Begins several years of graduate work and teaching in German and biology at various universities: Columbia, M.I.T., Johns Hopkins, University of Washington, and University of California–Berkeley.
1922	Otto Plath begins teaching at Boston University, where he progresses from an instructor of German to professor of biology.
June 1924	Aurelia Schober graduates as salutatorian from Winthrop High School, Massachusetts.
Fall 1924	Aurelia Schober enters Boston University as a freshman.
1925	Otto Plath earns M. S., biology, Harvard University.
1928	Aurelia Schober graduates valedictorian of Boston University's College of Arts and Letters.
	Otto Plath earns Ph. D., Harvard. His dissertation is *Bumblebees: Their Life History, Habits, and Economic Importance, with a Detailed Account of the New England Species.*
Fall 1928	Aurelia Schober teaches English and German at Melrose High School, Massachusetts.
1929	**Stock market crashes, beginning the Great Depression.**
Fall 1929	Aurelia Schober begins masters program at Boston University, enrolling in Otto Plath's Middle High German class.
September 1931	Aurelia Schober begins teaching German at Brookline High School, Massachusetts.

4 January 1932	Otto Plath files for divorce from Lydia Bartz and marries Aurelia Schober at Carson City, Nevada. Aurelia resigns from her teaching position at Otto's insistence.
27 October 1932	Sylvia Plath is born in Jamaica Plain, Massachusetts.
1934	Otto Plath's book, *Bumblebees and Their Ways*, derived from his dissertation and heavily edited by Aurelia, is published by Macmillan.
27 April 1935	Warren Joseph Plath, the poet's brother, is born.
1936	Plath family moves to Winthrop, Massachusetts, close to Aurelia's parents, primarily because of Otto's poor health.
September 1937	Sylvia starts first grade at Sunshine School in Winthrop, Massachusetts.
September 1938	Sylvia starts second grade at Annie F. Warren Grammar School in Winthrop.
21 September 1938	**The Great New England Hurricane of 1938.**
12 October 1940	Otto Plath's leg is amputated.
5 November 1940	Otto Plath dies.
7 December 1941	**Japan attacks Pearl Harbor; the United States enters World War II.**
Fall 1942	Aurelia moves with Warren, Sylvia, and the Schobers inland to Wellesley, Massachusetts. Sylvia is held back to fifth grade to attend school with children closer to her age. She begins Marshall Perrin Grammar School.
September 1944	Sylvia starts seventh grade at Alice L. Phillips Junior High School (grades 7–9).
1945	**Atom bomb is dropped on Hiroshima and Nagasaki. The United Nations is formed.**
20 January 1945	Sylvia sees professional performance of Shakespeare's *The Tempest* with her mother and brother in Boston.
September 1947	Sylvia begins tenth grade at Gamaliel Bradford High School. She attends Wilbury Crockett's advanced English class in American literature.
1949	Sylvia becomes editor of the high school newspaper, *The Bradford*, and writes column for *The Townsman*.
1950	**Senator Joseph McCarthy begins Communist "witch hunt."** **First organ transplant.** *I Love Lucy* **begins on television.**

	Korean War, 1950–1953.
	Sylvia performs in the high school production of J. M. Barrie's *The Admirable Crichton*. She publishes her first short story, titled "And Summer Will Not Come Again," in *Seventeen*. A poem, "Bitter Strawberries," appears in the *Christian Science Monitor*.
June 1950	Sylvia wins scholarship to Smith College, Northampton, Massachusetts. She attends on a scholarship from popular author Olive Higgins Prouty.
28 September 1950	Begins freshman year at Smith.
1951	***Catcher in the Rye*, by J. D. Salinger, published. Marianne Moore's *Collected Poems* published.**
1952 ·	**Princess Elizabeth becomes queen at age 25. Television's *American Bandstand* debuts.** Sylvia's short story "Sunday at the Mintons" wins prize and is published in *Mademoiselle*.
1953	***Playboy* magazine debuts with Marilyn Monroe on the cover. Arthur Miller's *The Crucible* opens.**
January 1953	Sylvia breaks her leg while skiing in Saranac, New York.
June 1953	Sylvia wins guest editorship at *Mademoiselle*; goes to New York City for one month and works as guest managing editor.
19 June 1953	**Rosenbergs are executed for alleged espionage.**
24 August 1953	Sylvia attempts suicide after learning that her application to Harvard's fiction writing course is rejected.
September 1953	Sylvia is treated by Dr. Ruth Beuscher at McLean Hospital, Belmont, Massachusetts.
1954	**The Supreme Court overrules "separate but equal" doctrine in *Brown v. Board of Education of Topeka* case. Ernest Hemingway wins Nobel Prize for Literature.**
February 1954	Sylvia returns to Smith.
Summer 1954	Sylvia attends Harvard summer school in Cambridge, Massachusetts.
1955	**Rosa Parks begins the Montgomery Bus Boycott by refusing to give up her seat on a bus. James Dean dies in car crash.**

January 1955	Sylvia submits her Smith College honors thesis, "The Magic Mirror: A Study of the Double in Two of Dostoevsky's Novels."
June 1955	Sylvia graduates summa cum laude from Smith College.
October 1955	Sylvia goes to Cambridge, England, on a Fulbright Scholarship to Newnham College, Cambridge University.
1956	**Allen Ginsberg's *Howl* published.**
26 February 1956	Meets Ted Hughes at a party and they begin a passionate relationship.
16 June 1956	Sylvia and Ted are married.
Summer 1956	Sylvia and Ted go to Wellesley, Massachusetts; Spain; and Yorkshire.
October 1956	Sylvia and Ted move to Eltisley Avenue, Cambridge.
Spring 1957	Sylvia concludes her studies at Newnham and the couple moves to the United States.
Summer 1957	Aurelia Plath gives the couple a gift of a summer on Cape Cod.
September 1957	Sylvia begins teaching at Smith College but finds it drains her energy for writing.
October 1957	**The Soviet Union launches *Sputnik*, beginning the space race.**
22 May 1958	Teaches her last class at Smith and argues with Ted after finding him with a female student.
Summer 1958	Sylvia and Ted move into an apartment in Boston near Beacon Hill.
22 October 1958	Sylvia takes a job as a receptionist in the psychiatric unit of Massachusetts General Hospital in Boston. In the evenings, she takes a creative writing workshop with Robert Lowell at Boston University.
10 December 1958	Resumes private therapy with Dr. Ruth Beuscher.
1959	**A *Raisin in the Sun*, by Lorraine Hansberry, opens on Broadway; it is the first appearance on Broadway of work by an African American female playwright. *Goodbye, Columbus*, by Philip Roth, wins National Book Award.** **Barbie® doll debuts.**
June 1959	Sylvia becomes pregnant.

Summer 1959	Sylvia and Ted make a cross-country camping trip of the United States.
September– November 1959	Sylvia and Ted write at two-month residency at Yaddo Writers Colony, Saratoga Springs, New York.
December 1959	Sylvia and Ted return to England and establish a home in Primrose Hill.
1960	**Camelot debuts on Broadway.**
1 April 1960	Frieda Rebecca Hughes, Sylvia and Ted's daughter, is born.
October 1960	*The Colossus and Other Poems* is published. Plath is working on *The Bell Jar.*
November 1960	**John F. Kennedy is elected 35th President of the United States.**
1961	**Vietnam War begins, will last until 1975.** **To Kill a Mockingbird, by Harper Lee, wins Pulitzer Prize.**
February 1961	Sylvia's second pregnancy ends in miscarriage.
March 1961	Sylvia has an appendectomy.
July 1961	Sylvia and Ted vacation in France.
22 August 1961	Sylvia finishes *The Bell Jar.*
31 August 1961	Sylvia, Ted, and Frieda move to Court Green in North Tawton, Devon.
November 1961	Sylvia receives Eugene F. Saxton grant to work on a novel.
1962	**Who's Afraid of Virginia Woolf?, by Edward Albee, debuts.**
17 January 1962	Nicholas Farrar Hughes, Sylvia and Ted's son, is born.
April 1962	Sylvia writes poetry intensively.
June 1962	Sylvia explains car accident as a suicide attempt.
Late June 1962	Aurelia Plath arrives in England and stays until August 4.
July 1962	Sylvia discovers Ted's affair with Assia Wevill.
5 August 1962	**Marilyn Monroe found dead in Los Angeles, presumed suicide.**
September 1962	Sylvia and Ted go to Ireland, stay with poet Richard Murphy. Sylvia returns alone. Sylvia and Ted separate.
October 1962	In a burst of creativity, Sylvia writes at least 26 of the *Ariel* poems.
12 December 1962	Sylvia moves with the children to the upstairs apartment at 23 Fitzroy Road in Primrose Hill, London NW1, in the building where William Butler Yeats

once lived. Sometime that winter she completes the collection, *Ariel*, comprised of 41 poems.

Winter 1962   **The United Kingdom experiences the coldest winter in over a century.**
The pipes keep freezing, and lights and heat go on and off at 23 Fitzroy Road. Plath struggles in the apartment with her two children, ages 2–1/2 and 9 months; all are ill and have no telephone.

January 1963   Plath's first novel, *The Bell Jar*, is published in England under the pseudonym Victoria Lucas.

11 February 1963 Sylvia Plath commits suicide by carbon monoxide poisoning, placing her head in a gas oven while her young children are asleep, sealed away in their bedroom. She was 30.

22 November 1963 **John F. Kennedy is assassinated in Dallas, Texas.**

1965   *Ariel*, a collection of poems, many written in the fall of 1962, is published in England. Ted Hughes, who edited the collection, removed poems, added others, and reordered the rest in the manuscript from the way Sylvia had originally prepared it. Only 27 of the original 41 she had included were published, and a mixture of 40 poems appeared in all.

1966   *Ariel* is published in the United States with 43 poems, again edited by Hughes.

1967   *The Bell Jar* is published in the United States under Sylvia Plath's name. A second edition of *The Colossus* is also published.
Assia Wevill gives birth to Shura, her daughter with Ted.

1969   Assia Wevill commits suicide and infanticide, killing Shura.

1970   Sylvia's unfinished novel, *Double Exposure,* "disappears."

February 1971   *The Bell Jar* is published in the United States under pressure of pirating. Aurelia Plath disapproves.
The poetry collections *Winter Trees* and *Crossing the Water* are published in the United Kingdom, including nine poems from Plath's original manuscript for *Ariel*.

1975   *Letters Home: Correspondence 1950–1963*, selected and edited with commentary by Aurelia Schober Plath, is published, partly in response to *The Bell Jar*.

1977	*Johnny Panic and the Bible of Dreams*, a collection of short stories, essays, and journal entries by Plath and edited by Ted Hughes, is published in the United Kingdom.
1979	U.S. publication of *Johnny Panic and the Bible of Dreams*, also edited by Hughes, with more inclusions than the U.K. edition. U.S. litigation occurs over *The Bell Jar* film.
1981	*Plath's Collected Poems*, edited and introduced by Ted Hughes, is published.
1982	Sylvia Plath wins Pulitzer Prize posthumously for *Collected Poems. The Journals of Sylvia Plath*, edited by Frances McCullough with Ted Hughes as consulting editor, is published.
1984	Ted Hughes is appointed poet laureate of England.
1987	Lynda Wagner-Martin's biography of Sylvia Plath is published in the United Kingdom
1988	Wagner-Martin's biography is published in the United States.
1989	*Bitter Fame*, by Anne Stevenson, allegedly written partly by Olwyn Hughes, Ted's sister, is published.
1995	Ted Hughes publishes his own *New Selected Poems 1957–1994*, containing five of the poems about Sylvia that will be part of *Birthday Letters*.
February 1998	*Birthday Letters*, by Ted Hughes, poems about his relationship with Sylvia Plath, is published. Sylvia's fans object to the publication of the collection in the month of Sylvia's death rather than her birthday month of October. They do not know that Hughes is dying.
Summer 1998	*Howls and Whispers*, by Ted Hughes, containing 11 new poems about Sylvia, is published in a limited edition of only 110 copies.
28 October 1998	Ted Hughes dies one day after what would have been Sylvia's 66th birthday. He was 68.
1999	A memorial stone is placed in Westminster Abbey's Poet's Corner in honor of Ted Hughes.

Birthday Letters wins the Whitbread Prize, Book of the Year Prize, T.S. Eliot Poetry Prize, and the South Bank Award for Literature.

2000   *The Unabridged Journals of Sylvia Plath*, edited by Karen V. Kukil, is published in both the United Kingdom and the United States. The edition contains twice the amount of material published in the 1982 edition, which was only published in the United States.

Ted Hughes archive is opened to scholars at Emory University, Georgia.

2003   *The Collected Poems of Ted Hughes* is published.

Fall 2003   *Sylvia*, film starring Gwyneth Paltrow as Sylvia and her mother, Blythe Danner, as Aurelia Plath, is released.

Fall 2004   *Ariel: The Restored Edition: A Facsimile of Plath's Manuscript, Reinstating Her Original Selection and Arrangement* is scheduled to be published.

Chapter 1

WHO WAS SYLVIA?
BEYOND THE ICON

As the twentieth century recedes, students and scholars of the twenty-first century will analyze those one hundred years to determine this time period's contributions to fields such as history, art, and literature. Time will tell who the "canonized" poets and novelists of the 1900s will be, but one candidate in contention for the list of important American poets of the age is certainly Sylvia Plath. Plath wrote in the post–World War II era of the 1950s and early 1960s. In the early years of the new century, Sylvia Plath's status as a serious poet remains threatened by her status as a cult icon, a cloud that has surrounded her reputation since she committed suicide in 1963 at the age of 30. While the cult figure lives on in the imaginations of those enthralled by mystery and tragedy, the serious poet has yet to universally establish herself in the minds of critics as a great writer partly, some would argue, through no fault of her own.

After her death, Plath's husband, Ted Hughes, who went on to become Britain's poet laureate, raised their two children and also controlled his late wife's estate and publications. Hughes edited and published several works by his wife posthumously, including her copious journals. Not unlike the editing of Emily Dickinson's work after her death, Hughes's choices in editing came under intense scrutiny in the years following his wife's death and were deemed problematic by many readers, scholars, and critics. These years coincided with the feminist movement of the 1970s and 1980s that echoed through not only American culture but also literary criticism of works by women. In the early 1980s, for example, when Hughes refused to publish all of his wife's journals, saying that he destroyed one of them to protect his children and another was "lost," feminists and others accused Hughes of man-handling and manipulating Plath's work and legacy, and even worse, silencing her voice.

Largely in response to Hughes's behavior after Plath's death and the decades that followed, feminist biographers and others began to blame Plath's depression and even her final act on Hughes's infidelity and ambition. The mythology over what happened in Plath's last months and days grew to such proportions that it threatened to overshadow the poetry. Since Ted Hughes's death in 1998, and the opening of his archives at Emory University in Atlanta, Georgia, in 2000, interest in the Plath-Hughes story has renewed, bringing editors, scholars, and biographers to the study of the newly available papers of both poets to try to come to a better understanding of what happened in their lives and how these events affected their work. Increasingly as time moves on, their lives and works are often considered in tandem to one another as though they are inescapably intertwined. Some argue that one cannot fully study the work of one poet without at least taking into account the work of the other.

At the same time, new editions of Plath's writing are clearing the way for fresh approaches to analysis of her poems and prose in their own right. For example, *The Unabridged Journals of Sylvia Plath*, which replaces sections omitted by Ted Hughes in the published journals of 1982, attempts to put Plath's work back in its original context. *Ariel*, Plath's posthumous and most critically acclaimed collection of poems, was scheduled to be published in late 2004 in a "Restored Edition," a facsimile that replaces the poet's original poems and ordering as she had them in manuscript form before the collection was heavily edited by her husband. With these efforts and others, Plath's work will be restored closer to its original condition. Most likely then it will be reassessed for its value and relevance to a new century.

As of early 2004, Sylvia Plath's poems continued to be anthologized in literature textbooks and other readers. While extensive, serious study of her work was not universally practiced in universities across the country, Plath was still generally regarded as an important poet with an intense voice that speaks to the conditions of females in the mid-twentieth century as well as other important themes such as family, nature, the Holocaust, and death. An Internet Web search in early 2004 yielded 127,000 Web pages devoted to the poet; a search of the Modern Library Association Bibliography yielded more than 200 books and articles about her and her work. Comparing these numbers to the more than 500,000 Internet hits and nearly 800 books and articles for the established canonical poet Emily Dickinson gives one a snapshot in time of the growing but relatively smaller scholarly and general reader interest in the more recent writer. With the new publications, these numbers are bound to increase as Plath's place in the literary canon in the academy is reevaluated based on more authentic editions of her work.

Cult iconic status of the poet aside, Sylvia Plath's work would not have received the attention it has so far without its devoted proponents among the literary establishment. Ted Hughes himself, who went on to have a long literary career lasting well over 30 years after his first wife's death with several published books and many accolades and awards, was first in line among the group to sing her praises. He claimed in a personal letter to the poet's mother soon after Plath's death that "no other woman poet except Emily Dickinson can begin to be compared with her."[1] Indeed, in her copy of *Understanding Poetry*, an anthology edited by Cleanth Brooks and Robert Penn Warren, Plath underlined the entire first stanza of Dickinson's poem "After great pain a formal feeling comes":

> After great pain, a formal feeling comes—
> The Nerves sit ceremonious, like Tombs—
> The stiff Heart questions 'was it He, that bore,'
> And 'Yesterday, or Centuries before'?[2]

She also underlined Brooks's commentary in the chapter, "...pain is a constant part of the human lot."[3] With most readers agreeing that Plath wrote her best work in October 1962, after her separation from Hughes and in the months following while living with depression in a cold apartment with two children under three years old; perhaps it did indeed take the pain of true suffering for her to reach the "bloodjet" she called poetry.

Publicly, Hughes also spoke highly of his first wife's poetry. In one of the first written comments about the *Ariel* poems that set the tone of criticism about the collection for some time, he wrote, "Behind these poems there is a fierce and uncompromising nature. . . . *Ariel* is not easy poetry to criticize. It is not much like any other poetry. It is her. Everything she did was just like this, and this is just like her—but permanent."[4]

A. Alvarez is a poet and critic who knew Plath in England. He also struggled with depression and attempted suicide; he accompanied Hughes to the coroner's office and funeral of the poet, and he was also an early advocate, especially of the *Ariel* poems. He made a memorable review of them on the BBC in 1963, and his subsequent writing and speaking on Plath and her work has kept him regarded as an authority on the subject ever since. M.L. Rosenthal's grouping of Plath's work in the "confessional" mode stuck for many years. Poet Robert Lowell, with whom Plath studied, described the author of the *Ariel* poems problematically as "hardly a person at all, or a woman, certainly not another 'poetess,' but one of those super-real, hypnotic, great classical heroines."[5]

Throughout the 1960s, critics considered Plath a "significant, if not yet major writer."[6] Critic Mary Ellman anticipated the surge of feminist interest in the 1970s when she focused on Plath's portrayals of the female body. The seventies drew enough interest that the first full-length study of the poet's work emerged, Eileen M. Aird's *Sylvia Plath: The Woman and Her Work* (1973) and the first collection of critical essays and reviews, *The Art of Sylvia Plath* (1970), edited by Charles Newman, which includes an essay by poet Anne Sexton, "The Barfly Ought to Sing." Attention to the poet grew after 1982 when her *Collected Poems* received the Pulitzer Prize. Following the first publication of her journals and collected poems in the early 1980s, Plath studies of the 1980s and 1990s developed in three major areas: feminist readings, cultural materialism that considered Plath's themes of the self and the world, and psychoanalytical readings of both her poetry and prose.

In the new century, as Plath's work gets reissued in editions that strive to be faithful to the poet's original intent, and as critics reevaluate it on those terms, her biography is also undergoing revision. Many biographers once felt compelled to write her life story based on taking a side in the Plath-Hughes controversy—either the Plath reading (poet as feminist martyr, defiled in both life and death by her ambitious, unfaithful husband) or the Hughes reading (insane, ambitious, and jealous wife whose cult following debased the value of Ted's life and work to Sylvia's). Recent biographers—with increased access to papers from both sides and with a better informed context of mental illness as a disease—are coming to the conclusion that the fairest account most likely lies somewhere between these two poles. They recognize that however problematic the editorial choices Hughes made might be, his first wife's death was the result of clinical depression and mental illness, a disease that cannot and should not be "blamed" on anyone, regardless of what events may appear to have triggered her final breakdown. Diane Middlebrook, for example, examines the couple's relationship in her book, *Her Husband: Hughes and Plath—A Marriage* (2003). After describing the events and reasons for hurt and blame on both sides, she concludes: "Depression killed Sylvia Plath."[7]

Just as any person's life need not be defined by the cause of her death from an accident, cancer, war, or murder, the same may be said for the victim of mental illness and suicide. Sylvia Plath was more than a sick woman who ended her life in what some have claimed was a desperate call for help at a time when her marriage was breaking up. She was also a little girl who played with paper dolls, a brilliant student and a Girl Scout who earned badges and went to camp, a woman who enjoyed children and the ocean, a thrill-seeker who liked driving a red car fast and also found contentment at quieter times in her life, as everyone does. She played viola and piano, and she loved to draw and paint. Her journals and schoolwork are enlivened with colorful and humorous sketches. She painted flowers on furniture and spoke German. She was a beekeeper and a baker.

Syl, as she was often called by friends and Sivvie by her family, stood 5 feet 9 inches tall in her stocking feet and would slip those feet into size 9 shoes, a larger size that she found embarrassing. She had brown eyes and light brown hair that bleached naturally blond in the summer sun and was platinum when bleached artificially. She tanned easily and was photogenic. Her height and slender build, facial features, and meticulous wardrobe and grooming early in her life caused some to call her attractive, though perhaps not beautiful. She did not lack for dates in a time (the 1950s) when a date on a Saturday night was as important a weekly accomplishment for Smith College students as an A+ on a test. Her appearance, combined with her fate, mythology, and the treatment she received from men in her life in the opinions of some (others argue she was in complete control), has caused some popular culture enthusiasts to call Sylvia Plath the "Marilyn Monroe of literature."

Her voice was deep, rich, and cultivated, and when she read her poems on BBC radio, her tone dripped with attitude. She wrote right-handed in clear schoolgirl penmanship page after page in volumes of journals she kept all her life. In childhood and again in her later years, she wore her hair in very long braids, as an adult often braiding it in one thick plait at the back, and coiling it on top of her head, letting the bangs hang down in front. As a mother, she loved her children intensely.

Just who was Sylvia Plath? As a human being, she was all of these things and more. As a woman and a poet, she was complex and driven and torn. Many read her work as self-centered, overly ambitious, and angry, and many read her life that way, too. But as an intelligent, award-winning, attractive female poet with a husband she loved and who shared her interests and two healthy children, what could Sylvia Plath have possibly been angry about? Perhaps a closer look at the events of her life may help illuminate some of its darker shadows.

NOTES

1. Hughes letter to Aurelia Plath, March 15, 1963; qtd. in Diane Middlebrook, *Her Husband: Hughes and Plath—A Marriage* (New York: Viking, 2003), p. 218.

2. Qtd. in Cleanth Brooks and Robert Penn Warren, *Understanding Poetry: An Anthology for College Students* (New York: Holt, 1938), p. 470.

3. Cleanth Brooks and Robert Penn Warren, *Understanding Poetry*, p. 470.

4. Qtd. in Clare Brennan, *The Poetry of Sylvia Plath: Essays, Articles, Reviews*. Columbia Critical Guides. (New York: Columbia University Press, 1999), p. 24.

5. Qtd. in Brennan, *The Poetry of Sylvia Plath*, p. 27.

6. Brennan, *The Poetry of Sylvia Plath*, p. 31.

7. Middlebrook, *Her Husband*, p. 211.

Chapter 2

EARLY LIFE AND FAMILY (PRE-1932–1936)

Sylvia Plath was a first-generation German American on her father's side and a second on her mother's. Neither side of the family had deep roots in the United States, but both sides were full of optimism and subscribed to the ethics of hard work so common among immigrants and their immediate descendants. Their common German heritages and work interests brought Plath's parents together. Gradually, the intertwining of language, work, and love that her parents developed early in their relationship would form patterns of experience that Sylvia grew up to emulate in her own adulthood.

AURELIA SCHOBER PLATH

If the poet needed a couple to model a happy marriage after, she would have found it in her maternal grandparents, Frank and Aurelia Schober. Franz Schober was born in Bad Aussee, Austria. In 1894, when he was 14, he crossed the Alps into Italy and moved to a village near Venice. After two years, he moved from there to Paris and to London two years after that, where he worked at a hotel as a waiter. At the London hotel, he met Joseph Grunwald, a coworker who showed him a photograph of his sister Aurelia, then 16 years old. Franz was so taken with her image that he told Joseph right then and there that some day he would marry his sister.

Joseph moved to America and changed his last name from Grunwald to Greenwood, a name that would appear in *The Bell Jar* years later. In 1902, Franz joined him in Boston. Changing his first name to Francis, he would go by the nickname Frank. Frank lived in the boardinghouse Joseph

owned. One day he opened the door and there stood Aurelia Grun-
wald/Greenwood, freshly arrived in America from where she had been
living in Vienna. Though he had never met her before, he knew Joseph's
sister was coming to America and he remembered the photograph. Seeing
her standing there, Frank could not believe that she was even more beautiful in person, and he was smitten on the spot. Apparently, Aurelia was
pleased with her brother's friend as well because the couple immediately
began a romantic relationship.

Aurelia's father was not happy with Frank, but by July 3, 1905, the day
Aurelia turned 18, the age of consent in Massachusetts at that time, she
and Frank obtained a marriage license. They were married soon after on
July 20. Nearly nine months after that to the day, on April 26, 1906, the
couple had their first baby, a girl they decided to name after them both;
they called her Aurelia Frances Schober. This daughter would be gifted in
her own right and would later become the mother of a poet.

Within a few years, the family had settled at a ranch house at 892
Shirley Street, on the peninsula of Point Shirley, Massachusetts. The
house was situated at the end of a dead-end street with the Atlantic
Ocean behind the house and Boston Harbor on the other side of the street
and the peninsula. Deer Island, where a state prison was located, sat south
of the peninsula, visible both day and night. At this location, the Schober
family grew to include another daughter five years younger than Aurelia,
named Dorothy, and a son 13 years younger than Aurelia, named Frank Jr.
Frank Sr. worked as an accountant with the Dorothy Muriel Company,
doing investment work on the side. Ironically, after some of his own in-
vestments for the family went bad, Aurelia the elder took control of the
family's finances.

Aurelia the younger loved growing up on the ocean. She was a good
student and loved to spend long hours reading near the water during the
summer. Her reading included the likes of Dickens, Thackeray, Eliot,
Hardy, Hawthorne, Melville, and Henry James. She enjoyed the novels of
the Brontë sisters and Jane Austen, but her favorite writer of all was the
poet Emily Dickinson. Aurelia dreamed of becoming a writer herself. Life
at the ocean gave her so many topics to write about—picnics and rowing
out to sea, picking up finds the ocean threw in her backyard, including
mussel shells, dead sharks, and even a tea set. If her father had not so
strongly disapproved, Aurelia would very likely have followed her dream
with more persistence and enthusiasm.

Though her childhood was a happy one on Point Shirley, Aurelia did
face the discrimination that has so often plagued immigrant families in
the years before and after her time. The Schobers were proud of their Aus-

trian heritage and spoke German at home with their children until they entered elementary school. After the outbreak of World War I, it was a difficult time to be of German descent in the United States. Irish and Italian immigrants and their descendants in the nearby town of Winthrop did not take kindly to the Schobers and harassed the children verbally. Once, a student pushed Aurelia out the door of a school bus and onto the ground when no one was looking. Families of German descent learned to stick together through the hard times. Despite the occasional trying days, Aurelia triumphed in her studies, graduating in 1924 from Winthrop High School as salutatorian, second in her class.

That fall, though she wanted to enroll in Boston University as an English and German major, she resigned herself to her father's practical wishes and signed up for Vocational Studies. Her excellence as a student persisted, even in this program she did not favor, and she joined several activities, including the English Club, the Writers Club, the German Club, and Student Government. She was editor-in-chief of *Sivad*, her school's junior yearbook, and inscriptions under her picture suggest that she was not only thought to be efficient in the position but also well liked by her peers. In 1928, Aurelia graduated top in her class at Boston University's College of Practical Arts and Letters.

That fall, she turned away from her vocational training and took a position teaching English and German at Melrose High School in Massachusetts. The following year, she enrolled in Boston University's Graduate School of Liberal Arts, and it was there that she met Otto Plath, who was a professor of German. Schober asked him to be her academic adviser and also the reader of her master's thesis. Her thesis turned out to be "The Paracelsus of History and Literature," an examination of Swiss physician Paracelsus, a controversial figure sometimes argued to be the father of modern chemistry. The much older Otto Plath, tall and striking in front of the classroom and much fancied by his female students, got to know Aurelia well through his work with her as her advisor. Though secretly attracted to Aurelia's appearance and intelligence, Otto maintained a professional relationship with his student until the day after her last semester ended.

OTTO EMIL PLATH

Not far from Bad Aussee, Austria, where Aurelia Schober's father was born, Otto Emil Platt was born in Grabow, Germany, on April 13, 1885. He was the oldest of six children raised by Theodore Platt, a hardworking blacksmith, and Ernestine (Kottke) Platt, a homemaker who grew, as she aged, somewhat moody from the burdens of raising her six children while tending to an ulcer that would not heal on her leg. Seeing that the need for blacksmiths was decreasing as Germany headed further toward industrialization, Otto sailed to the United States aboard the S. S. *Auguste Victoria* from Hamburg on September 8, 1900, at 15 years old. The ocean crossing took a week, but Otto's arrival in New York Harbor left him so infatuated with the city that he decided to stay there for a while rather than head immediately to his grandparents' house in Fall Creek, Wisconsin, as he had originally planned.

Platt changed his name to Plath and lived with an uncle while clerking at his uncle's store and auditing English classes in a local grammar school. In one year, he was speaking English fluently, and in another he was ready to embark on obtaining a formal higher education in the United States. His grandfather John in Wisconsin agreed to help him finance his dream, on one condition. Otto must promise to join the Lutheran seminary, become a minister, and serve his community in that capacity. Otto agreed to these terms and moved in with his grandparents in Fall Creek, taking classes at a prep school in Watertown. In the fall of 1906, Otto enrolled in Northwestern College in Watertown, Wisconsin, majoring in classical languages. Graduating in 1910, Otto started at the Wisconsin Lutheran Seminary in Wauwatosa, but after only a few weeks, he became disillusioned with the church and quit, despite his grandfather's threats of serious consequences if he did so. His grandfather's response was swift and permanent. He disowned Otto from the family by picking up a pencil and ceremoniously crossing Otto's name out of the family Bible. To this day, less is known about the poet's paternal side of the family.

Newly cut off from family ties, but willing to strike out on his own, Otto moved to Seattle, Washington. There he taught German at the University Heights School while also taking advanced studies in the language at the University of Washington. After reading Darwin at Northwestern, Otto also developed an interest in biology. Over the next several years, he continued teaching and studying in both subject areas, earning an M. A. from the University of Washington in 1912, an M. S. from Harvard in 1925, and a Ph. D. in science from Harvard in 1928. Otto was devoted to his work, and this fact combined with his frequent relocating, curtailed his social life. Through a friend at Northwestern, Rupert Bartz, Otto met and married Lydia Clara Bartz, Rupert's sister. The marriage did not hold up, and the couple was together only a few months. They drifted apart without legally ending the marriage. Otto had moved on and so many years had passed with his being heavily engaged in his work that he barely remembered ever being married.

During these years as well, in 1922, Otto taught German at Boston University and progressed through the academic ranks. As his graduate studies in biology progressed, he moved from teaching as an instructor of German to an instructor of German and biology to finally becoming a professor of biology. During these same years, Otto was publishing his research on such biological subjects as the crossbreeding patterns of finches, life cycles of fly larvae that feed on the blood of nesting birds, and the life habits of bumblebees. Journals that published Plath's work included *The American Naturalist, Biological Bulletin, Psyche,* and *The Bulletin of the Brooklyn Entomological Society*. His doctoral dissertation was *Bumblebees: Their Life History, Habits, and Economic Importance, with a Detailed Account of the New England Species*. By the time Otto Plath found himself reading Aurelia Schober's master's thesis on Paracelsus at Boston University, he was well into his forties and also at work revising his dissertation for publication with the hope that his first book would firmly establish his promising career in the field.

After the spring semester ended in 1931, both he and Aurelia were no doubt feeling doubly relieved that the pressure of class work was over. When the pretty, 25-year-old former advisee came by his office to thank him for advising her as she readied herself to go out into the professional world, Otto, old enough to be her father at age 46, finally felt free from professional decorum to make his move.

PARENTS AND EARLY FAMILY YEARS

Otto Plath asked Aurelia Schober to go with him for a weekend year-end party at Joseph and Josephine Haskell's country home. Joseph Haskell was a colleague of Plath's. Though Plath was nearly twice Aurelia's age, she had been attracted to him through their professor-student relationship as well, so after thinking it over for a moment, she accepted. At the Haskells', Otto confessed his infatuation with Aurelia and even told her of his marriage long ago that had never been legally terminated. Aurelia was taken with his frankness and his obvious attraction to her, which she was just learning about for the first time after knowing him for several months. Over the following summer, while she worked as a business manager at a camp for underprivileged children in Pine Bush, New York, and Otto taught summer school in Boston, they entered into a regular correspondence in which they told each other of their backgrounds and family histories.

That fall, Aurelia returned to Boston and began teaching at Brookline High School. That season she and Otto spent a lot of time together. They went hiking, visited the Arnold Arboretum, and attended the theater. Their mutual interests deepened their relationship quickly; by Christmas they were discussing marriage. During their holiday break from teaching, the couple drove across the country to Reno, Nevada, bringing Aurelia's mother along as a chaperone. In Reno, Otto filed for and received a divorce from Lydia Bartz without her participation or agreement. They had not seen each other in over ten years. Finally, at Ormsby County courthouse in Carson City, Nevada, on January 4, 1932, the couple was married in a civil ceremony. Aurelia's mother went with them while they took a short trip around Nevada as a honeymoon before heading back east.

When they returned to Boston, Aurelia moved into Otto's six-room apartment on the first floor of 24 Prince Street in Jamaica Plain. The times, Otto's older age, their established pattern of he being the advisor and she the advisee perhaps all contributed to Aurelia's compliance with Otto's requests of her. He asked that she resign her teaching position at Brookline High School, even though she was in good stead to one day head up the German department there. He wanted her to be a fulltime homemaker, and he wanted to begin a family right away. Aurelia did quit her job, never going back after the holiday break, and just weeks later she was pregnant. She took up the time of her pregnancy at home by preparing a nursery, reading up on child care, and composing lists of names.

On October 27, 1932, Aurelia gave birth to the couple's first child, a girl, at Memorial Hospital on Stoughton Street. Physicians J.J. Abrams and Edwin Smith pronounced the eight-pound-three-ounce baby healthy and alert. In choosing the name, the couple looked over their list and settled on the girl's name they liked the sound of the best—Sylvia. They gave her no middle name. As two academics interested in language, they may have known that "Sylvia" originates in Latin and means "from the forest." If they knew it, it apparently did not play a part in their decision. Pasted inside the cover of her baby book is a clipping from the November 3, 1932, *The Observant Citizen*, which announces that date as St. Sylvia's Day. It also tells that St. Sylvia was the mother of St. Gregory, and the name has become popular again possibly due to a song frequently heard on the radio, "Who Is Sylvia?" The song is different from Shakespeare's poem, "Silvia," which asks the same question. The couple took the new baby home to Jamaica Plain, where Aurelia nursed and cared for her while Otto continued to teach, do his research, and write.

As a bright woman who loved books, Aurelia trusted her instincts and tried some alternative methods of baby care and child rearing that she learned about from her reading and the reading she and Otto did together. Though feeding babies on strict schedules and not coddling them when they cried in between feedings was common practice in 1932, Aurelia nursed Sylvia on demand and gave her lots of holding, time, and attention in between. She read *Educating Man*, by Friedrich Froebel, as well as the ideas of Maria Montessori, carefully recorded every physical development Sylvia made, and took her for regular checkups to the pediatrician. Sylvia developed normally, gaining weight appropriately, growing from 22 to 29 inches in the first 18 months, and crawling, then creeping, and finally walking around her first birthday.

Interestingly, Aurelia noticed from very early on what she interpreted to be her baby's apparent desire to talk. Among the records she kept of these early developments, she describes in detail Sylvia's efforts at language, which she claims began as early as six or eight weeks. Aurelia recorded her baby's trials and errors at making vowel-sound gurgles and coos, then consonant ones, with what appeared to her to be determined effort. She was convinced that her bright child, to whom she gave much attention and read books, was trying her best to speak to her as early as possible.

While she tended to Sylvia, Aurelia was also writing, fulfilling her dream from long ago in at least one aspect. Instead of working on the novels based on her parents' experiences that she had hoped one day to write, she was helping Otto revise his dissertation on bees to submit to a commercial publisher. Otto was not particularly talented at writing. Taking his technical text, Aurelia rewrote it for an audience of general readers with Otto fact checking the manuscript as she went along. The task took many long hours, but once the Plaths were finished with it, they were able to successfully sell the manuscript to Macmillan. The New York publisher brought out the book under the less academic title of *Bumblebees and Their Ways* in 1934.

Scholars are quick to point out that, for all her work in revising Otto's text and rewriting technical concepts into plainer language, Aurelia is not mentioned in the book as coauthor. Instead, Otto places her name at the conclusion of his acknowledgments:

> These acknowledgments would not be complete without mentioning the service of my wife, Aurelia S. Plath, who has aided me greatly in editing the manuscript and in proofreading.[1]

In reality, Aurelia was the ghostwriter of the book. In one of several scenarios between husband and wife that echo through their daughter's marriage later on, Aurelia helped her husband's career without receiving the appropriate level of credit for the work she did at the time. The book put Otto Plath on the map as a recognized expert on bees and their habits.

The text was a groundbreaking study in entomology used as a standard by biologists for many years and is still referenced today for the foundational information that it provides in the subject.

In the book's introduction, Otto explains his interest in bumblebees as beginning when he was a boy in Central Europe:

> The foundations of this book were laid during my early boyhood in Central Europe, after my interest had been aroused by the discovery that bumblebees make delicious honey. Having repeatedly observed the activities of a neighboring bee-keeper, I thought it might be possible to transfer bumblebee colonies to artificial domiciles, and thus have honey available at all times. This idea was carried out a few weeks later, and during that and the two following summers about twenty-five bumblebee colonies belonging to six European species, were placed in cigar-boxes and transferred to the family garden. The method employed in "transferring" these colonies was rather crude, and so it happened that I was sometimes severely punished by the more vindictive species. Although these early attempts to "keep" bumblebees were made primarily for the purpose of obtaining honey, they also yielded some valuable scientific by-products, for in this way I became intimately acquainted with many of the activities of these insects, one of my favorite pastimes being to watch the queen oviposit [deposit eggs].[2]

Otto goes on to explain how he spent several of the preceding summers between academic years studying different species of bumblebees and how he hopes to continue that practice. Notable for coming from parents of a future poet is this sentence that Otto wrote and presumably Aurelia rewrote:

> As is well known, they [bumblebees] obtain their food almost exclusively from flowers, with which, as we shall see, they have entered into an interesting interrelationship.[3]

It is just this interrelationship that has fascinated poets from before Emily Dickinson to after Sylvia Plath as a metaphor for so many aspects of the natural world and the human condition. Otto's daughter would later not only keep bees herself but also transform the "interesting interrelationship" of her and her father and her father's interest in bumblebees into a unique poetry of her own. Poems to consider in this context include "The Beekeeper's Daughter," "The Bee Meeting," "The Arrival of the Bee Box," "Stings," and "Swarm."

Just as the Plaths were putting the finishing touches to the book, Carl Murchison, chair of the psychology department at Clark University, asked Otto to write an essay for his forthcoming collection, *A Handbook of Social Psychology*. Otto agreed, but with his heavy teaching load and other work on the bees book, he found little time to go through the 50 books he pulled together as reference material for the essay. Instead, he asked Aurelia to read and make notes for the essay for him. Probably glad to have the intellectual stimulation of another project to work on at home while taking care of baby Sylvia, Aurelia not only read the texts and took notes but also wrote the first draft of the essay for Otto. Otto wrote the second draft from hers, but then Aurelia revised and polished the third draft. The essay, entitled "Insect Societies," appeared in Murchison's edited collection, which again helped further Otto's career, but this time with no mention at all of Aurelia Plath.

While all this work was going on, Aurelia discovered that she was pregnant again. On April 27, 1935, at Jamaica Plain's Faulkner Hospital, she gave birth to what would be the couple's last child. They named him Warren Joseph. To help alleviate the feelings of sibling rivalry evident in young Sylvia as she watched her mother nurse her brother, Aurelia began teaching her phonics, practicing with her the sounds of capital letters Sylvia laid out on the floor beside her. Sylvia caught on quickly, to the delight of her mother. Some observers have noted that this performance to keep her mother's attention created a very early equating of language and approval in Sylvia's mind, an equation that would stay with her all of her life. Aurelia read books to both children as they grew, gradually moving from nursery rhymes and fairy tales and poems to Dr. Seuss and A. A. Milne's *Winnie the Pooh*; from Robert Louis Stevenson to Grahame's *Wind in the Willows* and Spyri's *Heidi*; and from Lamb's *Tales from Shakespeare* to J.R.R. Tolkien.

Aurelia once described her memory of Sylvia first learning to read simple words. One day while she was out with the children, Sylvia was walking alongside Warren who sat in the stroller when the three stopped at a crosswalk. Sylvia pointed to the stop sign on the corner and said to her mother, "Look Mommy, POTS."[4] By the time she was four years old, Sylvia could read simple story books. By five, she was already writing simple but composed poems.

In 1936, after going back and forth in the summers from Point Shirley where her parents still lived and the city where Otto taught and worked on his research, Aurelia finally convinced Otto to move to Winthrop, just three miles away from her parents. At the stucco house on 92 Johnson Avenue, Aurelia had the proximity to the ocean and parents she loved, and she was much happier. She had already come to realize that the long years of Otto's bachelorhood and self-absorption in his work would prevent him from seeing the benefits of a social life or value much time away from his work to spend with family. Aurelia, however, missed having friends. At least in the suburbs, she could find a community of other mothers with young children. Sylvia and Warren took all of her time as they grew, and her dreams of one day writing novels took a back seat when challenged with the fascination she had for her children and the time required for raising them. Before long, Otto would make even more demands on her that pushed her own dreams for herself back even further.

NOTES

1. Otto Emil Plath, *Bumblebees and Their Ways* (New York: Macmillan, 1934), p. xii.
2. Plath, *Bumblebees and Their Ways*, p. 1.
3. Plath, *Bumblebees and Their Ways*, p. 2.
4. Qtd. in Sylvia Plath, *Letters Home: Correspondence 1950–1963*, ed. Aurelia Schober Plath (New York: Harper & Row, 1975), p. 20.

Chapter 3

THE GOLDEN SCHOOLGIRL
(1937–1955)

From Sylvia's days seeking her mother's approval by learning her letters while watching her brother nursing to the awards and accolades won at Smith College and elsewhere in the mid-1950s, academic performance and recognition for it became an important part of the poet's identity and sense of self. She began to question this model for obtaining attention and affection while in college through events described in her autobiographical novel, *The Bell Jar*. Before that time, however, many years of hard work and accompanying rewards had set the pattern firmly in motion. This way of living, along with a natural disaster, a family tragedy, and a personal breakdown, mark the school years of this poet. She never lived long enough to share and delight in her own children's successes at school or to help right the wrongs from her own life by putting academic achievements into a more balanced perspective.

ELEMENTARY SCHOOL

In the fall of 1937, Sylvia Plath, though not yet five years old, started half-day first grade at the Sunshine School, a private elementary school near where her family lived in Winthrop, Massachusetts. At first, Aurelia Plath was concerned that her daughter might be too young to begin school, but the half-day schedule, Sylvia's early reading ability, and the attendance of a neighbor she knew who was a little older convinced Aurelia to give it a try. Little Sylvia walked a short distance to school each morning, and by noon, she walked back and excitedly shared her morning's activities with her mother and brother over lunch. The teachers, in particular Hope Cusiter, the headmistress at Sunshine School, soon notified Aurelia that she had made the right decision in sending Sylvia to class. She was a quick learner and was handling school well. In the fall of 1938, Aurelia sent Sylvia to the public school for second grade at Annie F. Warren Grammar School in Winthrop. The program went all day, and the school was a much farther walk for young Sylvia, but she continued to excel in her schoolwork and earned both good grades and compliments from her teachers.

THE GREAT NEW ENGLAND HURRICANE OF 1938

Not long into Sylvia's second grade school year, on September 21, 1938, the town suffered a huge hurricane that blasted over New England beginning at 5 o'clock that morning. The storm was a category 3 hurricane with sustained winds of 121 miles per hour and gusts up to 186 miles per hour and is still regarded as one of the worst storms recorded in southern New England's history. By the time it was over, the region suffered 564 deaths and 1,700 injuries. Between the hurricane and the resulting flooding of rivers in several states, the area lost 8,900 homes, seaside cottages, and buildings with 15,000 houses damaged. New England fishing fleets took a catastrophic hit with more than 2,600 boats lost and another 3,300 severely damaged.

As the storm roared over Winthrop, Massachusetts, that day, Aurelia and the children hunkered down in Otto's downstairs study for three hours. As the easternmost suburb of Boston and with the storm approaching from the seaward direction, Winthrop was the hardest hit town in the Boston area. When Sylvia, her mother, and brother emerged from the house, the damage they saw around them was devastating and near-traumatic for the future poet. Telephone poles were snapped in half; boats littered the shoreline; and whole cottages floated in the harbor. Though their own home escaped severe damage, these images of a broken world reemerge later in Plath's writing. At not quite six years old when it happened, Sylvia likely never forgot enduring and surviving her first and only natural disaster.

Her sensitivities as a future artist showed themselves in other ways as well in her early school years. As she advanced through third grade and on into fourth at E. B. Newton, Winthrop's pre–middle school, Sylvia was drawing quite a lot, a talent that was noticed early on, and she had already been writing and responding to poems for some time. Her mother recalled seeing her visibly troubled by the rhythm of a poem after she read her "The Forsaken Merman" by Matthew Arnold. A poem she wrote at Christmas,

1937, an unrhymed couplet called "Thoughts," is the first one Sylvia apparently regarded highly enough to copy over and date to keep. By the fall of 1940, she was writing poems quite frequently, copying over, dating, and keeping such efforts as "Snow," "My Mother and I," and "Perils of Dew."

Performance took on another important element in Sylvia's life when her father became ill to the point of needing to spend his time at home after classes away from his lively young family. At this time, writing poetry became one of the chief means for Sylvia to obtain her father's attention and affection.

A FAMILY TRAGEDY

Beginning in the summer of 1935, Aurelia noticed that Otto's health was becoming poor. Not only had he lost weight unexplainably, but he also was quick to anger as though something were chemically off in his system. Otto was not one to go to the doctor, so Aurelia's requests that he do so went unheeded. By the fall of 1937, he could barely get through his work week of lectures, meetings with students and committees, research, and grading papers. He came home every evening completely exhausted. Still, he would not see a physician about his symptoms.

Otto's illness became so severe and his need for rest and quiet so extreme that Aurelia created an upstairs-downstairs arrangement in the house in order to cope. She and the children occupied the house fully when Otto was at work, but once he was home, he had full reign of the downstairs while she and especially the children remained predominantly in living quarters upstairs. If Aurelia or the children had any company, their guests had to come and go before Otto got home or else come for dinner on an evening when Otto would be staying late at work.

That this arrangement estranged the biologist from his children is an understatement. The children ate, dressed, occupied themselves, and went to bed upstairs while he worked, ate, or relaxed downstairs. Each evening after eating dinner at their small table in their playroom and after their father had his meal downstairs, they were allowed to come down for one-half hour of his time and attention. In an effort to cheer him up from not feeling well, Aurelia had the children recite poems for their father during this time, or sing, or do other kinds of performances for him. Once these were done, the routine was that Otto showed his appreciation by giving them each a hug, and Aurelia hustled them back upstairs to bed. Unless he was working outside in the garden, he rarely ever saw them, or especially ever touched them, even while he was at home with them.

Performing for her father in this way to obtain his attention and affection made young and sensitive Sylvia want to please him all the more. She would often write poems and recite them to him or make him a special drawing. One can only speculate, or read her poems, to begin to decipher what effect performing for this mysterious, "colossal" figure she barely knew must have had on the poet's life and her later attitudes toward men. With such limited, special "audiences" with him, her father's importance must have grown to immense proportions in her mind as a child. One of the poet's more famous poems and the title of her first collection, "The Colossus," is said to weave strains of these feelings through its lines. A poem she wrote near the end of her life, "Daddy," attempts to exorcise the heavy influence he had on her through his death more than through his life.

Otto's stubbornness about not seeking medical help came partly from witnessing a colleague's unpleasant death from lung cancer. Without the knowledge about cancer that doctors have in the twenty-first century, treatments back then rivaled the disease itself for discomfort and unpleasantness. People who would not die now did then; treatments did relatively little to combat the spread or effect of the disease and simply prolonged an inevitable death. Otto convinced himself that he had the same symptoms as his colleague and was determined to fight it out or die on his own terms without allowing the medical community to interfere with his fate.

In 1938 and 1939, Otto endured two bouts of bronchial pneumonia and asthmatic conditions and allergies. As the house became more of a hospital and Aurelia more a nurse, she occasionally sent Sylvia to her parents' house on Point Shirley to help ease the workload and commotion. From there, Sylvia wrote letters to her father and occasionally called him on the phone. In one such letter, written around Valentine's Day, Sylvia writes her father, hoping he is feeling better. She writes about colors, and each time she mentions the color, she writes the word in that color. She also enclosed a handmade valentine on a heart-shaped piece of paper.

In 1940, Otto's symptoms increased to include insomnia, a nagging thirst that could not be quenched, and severe leg cramps that doubled him over in pain until he grabbed his calves and called out. The scenes were hard to stand by and watch and listen to helplessly, and they frightened both Warren and Aurelia to the point that they never quite forgot what they were like years later. Young Sylvia continued to try to cheer up her father. Her Father's Day card to Otto in June 1940 bore the saying, "My Heart Belongs to Daddy." Finally, on a morning in August as Otto was preparing to go to class, he stubbed his toe on the bedroom bureau.

This small injury would seem minute compared to his other problems, except that during the day the stubbed toe did not lose its sting but instead
grew to be more painful. When Otto returned home, he removed his socks
and shoes to find that the toe had turned purple-black and red streaks of
infection had made their way up his leg. Baffled that these symptoms appeared to have no relation to the lung cancer he was sure he had, Otto finally consented to allow Aurelia to call their family physician, Dr.
Abrams.

Abrams came to the house and examined Otto and took blood and
urine samples. He promised a diagnosis as soon as possible. The diagnosis
turned out to be diabetes mellitus, for which, even in 1940, treatment was
available that allowed patients to live long and fulfilling lives. The diagnosis, while startling to Aurelia, made sense with all of the symptoms she
knew Otto to have, including his insatiable sweet tooth (recall his admission in the introduction to *Bumblebees and Their Ways* that his interest in
bees began from the desire, as a boy, "to have honey available at all
times"). The problem was that Otto had ignored his condition for so long,
10 years altogether, that treatment was no longer possible, and the disease
was now fatal. Even if he had sought help a year or two before, Dr. Abrams
told Aurelia, there would have been treatments available that would have
kept him alive and living a fairly normal life. Otto Plath's refusal to seek
medical help and his stubbornness in mistakenly believing that his body
was fighting cancer all those years would soon take away a husband who
was the chief breadwinner of the family and the father of two children.

With what little time he had left, Otto fought to see if he could resur-
rect his chances by going on a strict diet and taking massive doses of insulin. During the course of this, he again contracted pneumonia and had
to be hospitalized in Winthrop Hospital for two weeks. Because of his feelings about the medical profession, Otto had never taken out health insurance, so the costs kept rising and rose even more when he returned home
from the hospital and required daily nursing care from a professional. On
one of the nurse's days off, Otto urged Aurelia to take the children to the
beach, assuring her that he was feeling especially well. Aurelia hesitated,
but finally took Sylvia and Warren outside. While they were gone, Otto
had a burst of energy that took him outside to look at the flowers in his
garden. While there, he got lightheaded and came back indoors; he was
trying to climb the stairs to his bedroom when he passed out.

Aurelia got uneasy leaving Otto alone, so she asked a friend to watch
the children and went back to the house. There she found Otto unconscious and sprawled on the stairs and thought he was dead. She rushed
over, shook him and patted him on the cheeks to revive him, and some-

how managed to get him up the stairs to bed. Seeing his condition—dry mouthed, a bright red face, and eyes twitching back and forth, it took a determined resolve on Aurelia's part to take a deep breath and draw up enough strength to help her husband for his sake and the children's. All night long, Otto sweated so much that his pajamas and bed linens needed frequent changing. In the morning, Aurelia took him to Winthrop Hospital, where Dr. Harvey Loder, a diabetes specialist, notified the couple that Otto's leg was gangrenous and needed amputation right away to save his life. The operation was performed on October 12, 1940, two weeks before Sylvia Plath's eighth birthday.

At first, the operation seemed successful, and plans were set in motion to fit Otto for a prosthesis. Soon, however, Otto began to decline, and Aurelia tried to stay with him at the hospital as much as she could. Otto seemed to know the end was near. On November 5, 1940, he told his wife that he really did not mind dying that much except that he would have liked to have seen the children grow up. Aurelia thought it was unlikely that a man 55 years old could die. She decided to go home and clean herself up that evening so that she could be refreshed to deal with her husband's concerns in the morning. As soon as she reached the door and was unlocking it, however, she heard the telephone ringing inside and feared the worst. The doctors informed her that not long after she left, Otto suffered an embolism to his lung, which killed him instantly. They told her he died so quickly that he probably never knew it was happening.

Sylvia and Warren were asleep upstairs, so Aurelia decided to wait until the next morning to tell them. Sylvia was sitting up in bed reading a book when her mother went into her room. The little girl's immediate reaction to the news of her father's death was, "I'll never speak to God again."[1] Then she threw her blanket over her head.

Aurelia made what may have been a crucial mistake in not taking the children to their father's funeral and in not encouraging them to outwardly grieve. She thought they were too young, and this was before the time of grief counseling for families or much emotional or psychological support was available to help with feelings of loss. There is a photograph among Plath's papers of Sylvia wearing a nurse's uniform given to her by her father's nurse. She sits on the ground in front of the flowers her father planted. She looks at the camera wearing the starched white dress and classic hat. Beside her are her doll "patient" and a blanket. Aurelia had a friend babysit the children while she and her parents attended Otto's funeral at the First Methodist Church in Winthrop. Reverend Harry Belmont Hill officiated. Otto was buried in the Town Cemetery, Grave Number 1123, which lay next to the cemetery's Azalea Path. The similarity of the path's name to her mother's would not be lost on the poet years later. After the burial, Aurelia Plath returned home and tried to pick up the pieces and begin a new life. She did not take her children to visit the grave.

Not only did Aurelia lose the primary breadwinner for her family at Otto's death, but her father Frank also lost his job at the Dorothy Muriel Company to early retirement due to company downsizing about the same time. The families decided to pool their resources. "Grammy" and "Grampy," as Sylvia and Warren called their maternal grandparents, moved in at 92 Johnson Avenue. Grammy Schober cooked, cleaned, and took care of the children while Aurelia taught German in a temporary position at Braintree High School for the spring 1941 term.

For the fall, Aurelia was offered a permanent position at Winthrop Junior High School, teaching ninth grade but also supervising the school's accounting system. Already physically hurting with a duodenal ulcer that developed during the constant stress and vigilance of Otto's care, Aurelia worried about the accounting duties for the school on top of teaching, but she took the job anyway because she needed the money for her family. Apparently Otto had not believed in insurance of any kind because not only had he no health insurance for himself, but he also left behind no life insurance to help his family with expenses after his death.

Sylvia and Warren became sick with normal childhood illnesses soon after Otto's death. They both got the measles, Warren contracted pneumonia, and Sylvia began a chronic struggle with sinusitis that gave her severe headaches all of her life. Later both children developed tonsillitis and had their tonsils removed. Despite her family's traumatic experience, the reshuffling of living arrangements, and her own illnesses, Sylvia continued to do well in school.

It appears that writing became one of her therapeutic outlets at about this time. Unusual for one so young, Sylvia began sending out her poems to newspapers and magazines (probably with Aurelia's urging and help). On August 11, 1941, nine months after her father's death, young Sylvia Plath had her first publication. She was eight years old. It was a poem called "Poem," published in the children's section of the *Boston Herald*. A verse about crickets and fireflies, the commentary from the child author below the poem read, "I have written a short poem about what I see and hear on hot summer nights."[2]

In addition to her writing, Sylvia enjoyed spending time on the beach and watching the airplanes fly overhead going to and from Boston's Logan Airport. She could see the airport across the harbor from her bedroom window in Winthrop. By the time the Japanese attacked Pearl Harbor before Christmas in 1941, Sylvia was already sensitive to the approach of war and planes, and there began another hard road for Germans and their descendants in the States. Later, in a short story she wrote about a family gathered around the radio, she recounts the mother whispering that she is glad her husband did not live long enough to see things come to this.

As Aurelia worked hard to support the family, the stress of that as well as dealing with her own grief and the toll of having cared for Otto during his long illness and on top of all this the onset of the war caused her ulcer to act up more than ever. In the summer of 1942, soon after her brother Frank married and went off to war, she was invited by Boston University's College of Practical Arts and Letters to develop and oversee a new program for medical secretaries. The position offered higher pay, and Aurelia knew university teaching would be less stressful for her, so she accepted.

With this change came another decision. Aurelia thought it might be best for the family to leave Winthrop. She thought the ocean aggravated her arthritis that was just beginning and made Sylvia's sinusitis and Warren's respiratory infections worse. Perhaps most important, she decided she wanted her children to grow up in a community that offered a higher concentration of educated people and professionals as opposed to blue-collar workers. As she looked around for a new place, she studied the town of Wellesley. She liked the college town and found out that as a member of the community, Sylvia would have the opportunity to attend Wellesley College, one of the highly regarded Seven Sisters women's colleges in New England, on full scholarship, a quality education that Aurelia knew she could never afford to give her daughter on her salary.

By Sylvia's tenth birthday on October 27, 1942, the family sold the house in Winthrop and was moving to 26 Elmwood Road in Wellesley, leaving the sea both mother and children loved so well and their wonderful experiences there behind. It was a watershed moment for Sylvia as well, who recounted later, "And this is how it stiffens, my vision of that seaside childhood.... My father died, we moved inland. Whereupon the first nine years of my life sealed themselves off like a ship in a bottle—beautiful, inaccessible, obsolete, a fine, white flying myth."[3]

It does not seem to most observers that enduring the death of a parent would make a young childhood idyllic, and Sylvia had not lived all of that time by the sea, having spent her first four years in Jamaica Plain, but the ocean definitely had a calming effect on her mother and her family that continued to work its charm on Sylvia through her adolescence and young adulthood. In her high school scrapbook, Sylvia relates that it is difficult to express just how much the ocean means to her—that it seems as though it were a person's "spirit," a presence, and an important part of her "heritage." Rather than a romanticized image of an idyllic childhood, perhaps the years sealed off like a ship in the bottle, for her, served more as a forerunner of another glass enclosure, the bell jar.

JUNIOR HIGH SCHOOL

Rather than enroll Sylvia in the sixth grade when they arrived in Wellesley, Aurelia thought it was a good time to close the gap in age between Sylvia and her classmates. Since she had begun school so early, she was two years younger than most of her classmates. Keeping Sylvia in the fifth grade at Wellesley's Marshall Perrin Elementary School would close the gap by one year. There Sylvia built her confidence and made friends. Since the academic load felt lighter to her, she had the time to take piano lessons and participate actively in her new Girl Scout troop and make new friends there, at school, and in the neighborhood. Both she and her mother made important friendships in their early time at Wellesley.

Missing the ocean for her reveries and walks, Sylvia began to enjoy spending time climbing and sitting in the apple tree in the backyard. The woods nearby provided another play space for her and a neighbor friend, 10-year-old Betsy Powley. There was a little brook running through it, and there the children built a hut out of ferns where they would go to talk and laugh or read. Aurelia became friends with Mildred Norton and her family. Mildred was the wife of a colleague of Otto's, and her three boys provided companionship for Warren and Sylvia when the two women visited each other back and forth.

Sylvia's reading and writing accelerated in Wellesley as she moved into adolescence. When she did enter the sixth grade at Alice L. Phillips Junior High in the fall of 1943 at age 11, she read so many books that year that she received a special certificate from the Massachusetts Division of Public Libraries' Department of Education. In junior high, her activities included basketball, serving as vice president of her homeroom and as class volunteer for the selling of Defense Stamps, a fundraiser to support the war effort.

Her activities outside of school included enjoying the popular radio programs "The Jack Benny Show" and "The Lone Ranger." In late 1944, her Aunt Dorothy ("Aunt Dot," Aurelia's sister) took her and Warren to see the movie *Lassie Come Home* starring Roddy McDowall and Elizabeth Taylor. Other movies included *The Scarlet Pimpernel*, *Riding High*, and *Jane Eyre*. Her childhood diaries indicate that she and her mother enjoyed *Jane Eyre* so much that they sat through it twice in a row, and Sylvia then read the book. About this time she also began attending various social functions with boys. Even though she also liked music and art, sun-bathing, reading, and writing remained her primary interests. When summer arrived at the end of sixth grade, Sylvia celebrated by lying out in the sun rereading *Gone with the Wind* in two days, her third time through the book.

Her writing at this time included a short story called "The Thrilling Journey of a Penny." She also outlined a novel that was going to be narrated by a character named Nancy. Poems written during her junior high years include verses she would later call "jingles" such as "In the Corner of My Garden" and "A Wish upon a Star." *The Phillipian,* the school newspaper, regularly published her poems and also her drawings. During this time she also began organizing her poetry, building poem after poem at a quick pace. She kept three separate books in which to keep work she had copied over and dated or other writing or clippings she wished to save—one was a scrapbook; one was a diary; and one was a book she called her *Life Poem Book.*

Her famous habit of chronicling seemingly every detail of her life in diary or journal form appears to have begun around this period as well. Her early diaries, such as the dated 1944 and 1945 books, are filled to capacity with information about her classes and assignments; books she was reading; achievements in school; piano and viola lessons; meetings and badges she was working on in Girl Scouts; small sketches; and details about playing with friends. Typically, she kept to the one page per date design of the first printed diaries, but occasionally her entries squeezed over onto the next day, such as her account of her Girl Scout troop's Court of Awards celebration on May 22, 1944. There she proudly writes of the occasion when she received 10 hard-won badges she had been detailing the progress of all along in her daily entries: World Knowledge, Scribe, Readers, Child Care, Bird Finder, Group Music, Campcraft, Foot Traveler, Boating, and Weaving. In July 1947 she writes that she and Aurelia go shopping at Ward's in Winthrop, where she selected an undated journal from the stationery department in which she could finally take all the room she liked to record her days and thoughts.

Unlike her published adult journals, thus far Plath's childhood diaries and journals have gone underutilized in the story of her development as a woman and a writer, as well as for the potential contributions they might make to understanding girlhood in middle twentieth-century New England. As study of the century develops over time, publishing these materials might be of use to historians and scholars as well as to Plath enthusiasts. The young Plath records movies she saw, funny books (comics) she and "Warrie" collected and read, as well as other activities she engaged in with her friends in her spare time. The diaries not only reveal information about Plath the young poet but also about popular culture in the time of a 1940s American teenager.

She writes enthusiastically of beginning a pressed flower scrapbook, for example, on May 20, 1944, and begins a weekly accounting of what kinds of flowers are on the church windowsills each Sunday. She writes of playing dolls with her friend, Betsy, and getting Bette Davis's autograph in scouts from the actress's aunt who visited her troop. She once sewed three buttons on the wrong side and an apron that was too wide for her in sewing class. Sunday nights she listened regularly to radio shows such as "The Great Gildersleeve" and "Jack Benny"; she saw a re-release of the Disney film *Snow White* on November 25, 1944. She writes of drinking Kool-Aid at her teacher, Miss Moore's, party and a glass of Ovaltine after reading and before going to bed at night. She ate Sugar Daddy candy bars and played card games like fish and board games like Monopoly and Uncle Wiggly. One day she jumped rope 109 times without stopping and found this accomplishment noteworthy to set down in ink. She records the day Franklin D. Roosevelt died, the day the bomb was dropped on Hiroshima, and the day World War II ended. Rarely has a life been so copiously documented as that of Sylvia Plath.

The diaries tell that Plath was an avid fan of paper dolls as a child and not only collected the popular versions modeled in the forms of movie actresses of the day such as Shirley Temple but also designed and drew her own paper dolls with vibrantly colorful clothing and accessories—dozens of which still exist in the archives. In a June 21, 1944, entry she describes staying home from day camp because it was raining and spending the day using a *Mademoiselle* magazine with her paper dolls. The irony of this childhood occupation considered in relation to her later experience with the magazine is almost palpable. Less than a decade later, as guest editor in college, she and the other guest editors would become "paper dolls" themselves for the magazine as they were not only expected to produce first-rate, publishable work as intern editors but they also had the additional burden of appearing in the same issue as fashion models and at events around New York City as publicity props.

Her development as a writer grows through the childhood diaries as well, from logs of months and seasons divided into the schedule of her school days, class by class and activity by activity, to longer entries about how she feels about boys and friends and teachers and books and thoughts about her future. Poems enter the diaries early on, and she writes of becoming inspired in the middle of the day and jotting down poems on the spot. As a stellar student, it appears she would not think of stopping her schoolwork for any other kind of purpose than to take advantage of such

instantaneous moments of creativity. As part of her regular English assignments, she was required to do recitations, and some of her choices of
readings are intriguing. On June 7, 1944, for example, she records reciting
Emily Dickinson's "Sunset and Sunrise" poem, which may have been the
poem now known by its first line, "I'll tell you how a sun rose."

Plath did not read only classics of literature among her own library
choices and those pressed on her by her mother and her teachers, but she
also seemed to favor several of the less critically acclaimed popular fiction
of her time such as *The Bobbsey Twins* and Judy Bolton mysteries. She
often received books as gifts for birthdays and Christmas (she typically put
lists of gifts received at the back of her diaries), and at one point she
boasts that her personal library had grown to 100 books. She often read in
bed at night when her mother did not know. At the same time, she was
taking note of images and events around her that would later resurface in
her mature writing, such as her friend Betsy's beautiful tulips pressed into
her flowers scrapbook or the gray, shadowy look of the moon during the
lunar eclipse she viewed from her home on December 18, 1945. In short,
the childhood diaries and journals show an ambitious, talented girl widely
interested in life and the world around her.

Readers of Plath's last poetry collection *Ariel* may find it interesting
that on January 20, 1945, Aurelia took Sylvia and Warren to see Shakespeare's *The Tempest* at the Boston Colonial Theater. Aurelia described
the evening and the children's responses to it in a note to herself at the
time. She said the snowstorm that was due held off, the play was spectacular, and the event was magical in every way. The children already knew
the story from Lamb's adaptation for children and by now had read the
original Shakespeare as well. Years before, they had lived through a real
tempest in the form of a hurricane at the edge of the sea and a figurative
tempest through their father's illness and death, which was still not discussed in the household. In her diary, Sylvia described the play as too perfect to be expressed in words and the day as one of the most profound of
her life, a day spent in a better world.

Twelve-year-old Sylvia sat transfixed in the audience as the spirit Ariel
was released by Prospero. "Ariel's Song" about the death of a father must
have rung particularly deep in her hearing that day and in her musings on
the train ride home through the winter landscape that evening. In the
song, Ariel sings of a father who lies a "full five fathoms" deep under the
ocean where his bones have turned to coral and his eyes to pearls:

Nothing of him that doth fade
But doth suffer a sea-change

Into something rich and strange.
Sea-nymphs hourly ring his knell.[4]

Perhaps the person's spirit she felt the ocean had when she wrote about it in her scrapbook was intertwined with the abrupt absence of her father while they lived at the ocean's edge. It would take many years and many trials, but eventually the poet would work her own "sea-changes" over her father's memory, turning it into something rich and strange and ringing his knell through her poetry.

For now, though, junior high school proceeded for her, and the war ended. Sylvia read the accounts of the bombing of Hiroshima on a layover during a train ride back with her mother from visiting friends in Maine. She remarked on it in her diary and was particularly shocked at the account that 60 percent of the city was demolished. Later she, like the rest of the country, would begin hearing the first stories of the Nazi concentration camps that were being found in Europe as the Americans began freeing prisoners and countries began recovering from the ravages of a long and brutal world war.

In her eighth grade year, Sylvia was elected homeroom president and read such novels as *Pride and Prejudice*, *The Scarlet Pimpernel*, and *Twenty Thousand Leagues under the Sea*. At camp that summer, she swam, worked at crafts, and picked blueberries. As a tall and growing adolescent, her appetite was voracious, and she wrote freely in her diaries about taking second and third helpings of foods such as soup, salad, potatoes, and cabbage and drinking up to seven cups of milk in one go. For the blueberry picking, she and her friends hiked two miles to the farm from camp, then picked all day, filling bushel baskets. Sylvia and her friend Ruth Freeman from Winthrop picked 20 quarts together, earning themselves a dollar each for extra camp expenses. Later that summer back in Wellesley, Sylvia decided it was time to go through her poems once again and copy over and repackage them chronologically. She copied over ones she wanted to keep into a composition notebook and illustrated them with crayon and ink drawings. She called her homemade anthology, *Poems by Sylvia Plath*. For the rest of the summer, when she was not working on her poems, she read more novels such as Dickens's *A Tale of Two Cities*, *Oliver Twist*, and *David Copperfield*.

In Wellesley at this time, ninth grade was treated as the last year of junior high school. Sylvia continued to garner good grades and read and write. She adopted a pen pal from Germany, Hans-Joachim Neupert from Ruckersdorf, and in her letters to him she explained that she wanted to be a journalist, writer, or an artist when she was out of school and was working hard at her studies to be able to achieve her goals. At the end of the year, she was honored with several awards as she completed junior high school and prepared to move on to high school the following fall. These prizes included a fifth and sixth orange and black block "W" school letter; a commendation that stated she was the only student in the school's history to have earned enough credits for a sixth letter; a certificate from the Carnegie Institute for winning first place in a national art contest; commendations for high grades (all As and Bs); and a card for punctuality. On the last day of school, she passed her yearbook around as most students do, and she obtained 75 autographs of good wishes from her peers. The difference in this number from the scant few in her later senior year high school yearbook is striking and noteworthy.

One last award, for being a "special student," was a copy of *Understanding Poetry* edited by Cleanth Brooks and Robert Penn Warren, the very same copy that is housed in the rare book room at Smith College today and bears her copious underlining, including the first stanza of the Dickinson poem, "After great pain, a formal feeling comes." Her annotations in the book suggest that amid all the awards and accolades, boyfriends, friends, and activities, this bright, promising fourteen-year-old was connecting with a level of pain she apparently could explain to no one.

HIGH SCHOOL

For Sylvia Plath, Gamaliel Bradford High School was marked in her memory by ambition, accomplishments, and the existence of one very special teacher—Wilbury Crockett—who taught the advanced English classes of all three years. Tenth grade, he told his students on the first day, would cover American literature; their junior year they would study British titles; and world literature would be covered in their senior year. Because he taught advanced English students who would very likely be applying to Ivy League and Seven Sisters colleges around New England, Crockett took his college prep classes seriously and taught them like college seminars. The first year, he told Sylvia's class, they would read 45 major works including novels, long poems, and plays. Instead of tests, the students would write four 5,000-word essays, which they would read aloud standing in front of the class and then defend by answering questions. Some students hearing a challenge such as this become discouraged and turn away, and some students rise to the task. The day after Crockett laid out the demands of his class, only two-thirds of the students returned. Sylvia was one of those who believed Mr. Crockett was one who finally understood that superior students needed to be challenged to reach their full potential. To Sylvia, Wilbury Crockett was "the teacher of a lifetime."[5] If Crockett were such a teacher, then Sylvia Plath, out of many others he had helped get into Ivy League schools or on other roads toward successful futures before and after her, was the kind of student he had been waiting for.

Sylvia began writing to please her teacher right away, and please him she did. First, he read aloud a paraphrase assignment she had written and asked the class which of those he had read, including hers, were the best. He agreed with a classmate who remarked that the best was Sylvia's. Next, he read two of his favorite poems of four she had handed in to him, "I Thought That I Could Not Be Hurt" and "Alone and Alive" and told the class that he thought she had a gift for writing lyrics. The former poem was about a small incident that happened at home. Grammy Schober accidentally smudged one of Sylvia's blue pastel still-life drawings. The loss, however minor to someone else, somehow cut Sylvia to the quick, and she dramatized her feelings in the poem. Though the poem was fairly sentimental, it demonstrated to Crockett that Sylvia had skill and seriousness in her poetry and the desire to find and write about the emotional truth of a situation. His praise did nothing but encourage her to write even more.

Sylvia's activities in high school included basketball, orchestra (where she played viola), and contributing articles to the student paper, *The Bradford.* She joined a high school sorority, the Sub-Debs for a short time, then dropped out when she noticed how members treated nonmembers. She went to formal dances and dated several boys. Though her studies and getting good grades were paramount to her, increasingly she had to fight the distraction of her growing sexual desire. She finished her sophomore year of high school again with awards and accolades. Her artwork again won a Carnegie Institute certificate for being part of an exhibition there. R. H. White presented her with the prize. Her writing flourished and developed with one effort in particular, "Youth's Appeal for Peace." Comprising several sections, it was her most ambitious poem to date.

By now, Girl Scout camp had given way to other summer experiences. For the second year, Sylvia attended a sailing camp on Martha's Vineyard. From her letters and other writing while away at this camp, it appears sailing did not interest her as much as being near the sea in general did. She loved to swim, sunbathe, and eat. Her appetite was still voracious, though she did not gain weight. After camp, Sylvia decided she had outgrown the experience and would only return as a counselor.

In the fall of 1948, Sylvia entered her junior year of high school, a year that then, as well as now, can be the most challenging for students academically. Her classes included English, Latin, French, American history, math, and art. She won an achievement key in the Scholastic Art Awards Competition in the spring and that same month composed with a class-mate a letter to respond to an article in *The Atlantic Monthly*. The article was written by Columbia University professor Irwin Edman and was titled "A Reasonable Life in a Mad World." Speaking on behalf of Wilbury Crockett's class, the "Crocketteers," Sylvia and her cowriter challenged the ideas in Edman's essay. Edman wrote back only a short note, recom-mending that the students wait until they entered college and consider his ideas again then in more depth. Late in the school year, when Sylvia was sporting all As in her classes, she was chosen coeditor with Frank Irish of *The Bradford*. For the second year, she received honorable mention in *The Atlantic Monthly's* annual student poetry contest. Sylvia's annual cycle of hard work, good grades, and activities culminating in prizes every spring had by now flown into high gear.

With the pressure of college admissions applications looming in her senior year, Sylvia applied herself with more determination than ever to her studies. She continued to read, write, and submit poems to magazines, while taking the course in world literature with Mr. Crockett, college bi-ology, U.S. history, French III, advanced art, and gym. Poems she wrote that year include "Adolescence," "Lonely Song," "Question," "White Phlox," "Gone Is the River," "The Farewell," and "City Streets." Her writ-ing career running alongside her studies kept up a steady pace with Crock-ett's encouragement. She submitted batches of poems to *Seventeen* and *Ladies' Home Journal* and one poem, "The Invalid" to *The Atlantic Monthly*. Over time, she sent 30 poems to *Seventeen* alone. She also sub-mitted a short story, "East Wind," to *Mademoiselle*. None of these works was accepted. Years later Aurelia would comment that many young writ-ers looked with envy at Sylvia as an instant success, when she had actu-ally received many rejections for her work but simply remained persistent in submitting. Several rejection slips from *Seventeen* alone still exist in the Plath archives. In *Letters Home*, Aurelia claims there were 45.

Though she knew that her chances of a local town scholarship to Wellesley were excellent, Sylvia began thinking about applying to Smith College, one of the premier women's colleges in the country. One hun-dred miles away from Wellesley in Northampton, Massachusetts, Smith would not only give her the quality higher education she sought, but it would also give her breathing space from her mother and her family. To save space in the house, she and Aurelia had shared a bedroom at 26 Elm-wood Road. Though Aurelia must have been concerned about how to pay for Smith should Sylvia be admitted, she allowed her to apply there as well as at the more certain Wellesley.

Sylvia's application resume for Smith included a listing of selected recent reading that presumably she thought would impress admissions officers. She grouped the listing by genre. Titles included Plato's *Republic*, Aeschylus's *Agamemnon*, Ruskin's *Sesame and Lilies*, Emerson's essays, A. E. Housman's *A Shropshire Lad*, Eliot's *The Waste Land*, Sherwood Anderson's *Winesburg, Ohio*, Thomas Mann's *Buddenbrooks* and *Doctor Faustus*, Thomas Hardy's *Return of the Native*, Edith Wharton's *Ethan Frome*, Undset's *Kristen Lavransdatter*, Huxley's *Point Counter Point*, Willa Cather's *My Antonia* and *Death Comes for the Archbishop*, and Lewis's *Main Street* and *Arrowsmith*. In addition to her reading, Sylvia emphasized her school awards and activities, including basketball and tennis, the yearbook staff, her Unitarian Church's Young People's Association (Aurelia had been brought up Catholic but joined the Unitarian Church in Wellesley), and the World Federalist Organization. Despite IQ tests throughout her school years that had scored the poet in the genius category, she received a 1267 score on the Scholastic Achievement Test (SAT), 700 in the verbal section and 567 in math. For references, she asked Mr. Crockett, neighbor Mrs. Duane Aldrich, and the principal of Bradford, Samuel Graves, to write letters. Graves indicated in his letter that Sylvia was a "superior candidate" for college and that "no one could be more eager for a college education." He also seemed to sense danger in Sylvia's level of ambition and possible future problems when he wrote, "May college mean some 'fun' for her as well as intellectual accomplishments."[6]

Both Wellesley and Smith, the only two colleges where she applied, accepted the high school senior into their incoming freshman classes of 1950. Sylvia was delighted with the Smith acceptance and continued to regard that school as her first choice. Now she and Aurelia had the task of finding enough financing for Sylvia to attend. Smith had offered her a scholarship, but her request for work study had been denied. Wellesley's Smith Club, an alumni group in town, gave her an additional scholarship, which brought the bill within a range Aurelia could afford, though not without significant struggle. When Sylvia graduated as valedictorian from Bradford High School on June 7, 1950, she crossed the stage to accept her diploma confident that she would be attending Smith in the fall.

The cycle of spring accolades and awards reached another threshold at her high school graduation. Sylvia graduated top in her class of 158 students. She was a member of the National Honor Society along with all of her other normal activities. That spring she tried out for a role in the senior play, *The Admirable Crichton*, by J. M. Barrie, and got the major role of Lady Agatha Lasenby. The play was directed by Mr. Crockett. Sylvia received third billing after the star and costar.

Not only had she achieved high school success in her last year of high school, but her writing was also getting serious attention in the "real world" of publishing at the same time. An essay she cowrote with a classmate from Crockett's class, Perry Norton, "A Youth's Plea for World Peace" was accepted for publication in *The Christian Science Monitor* in March. The same day she heard this news, Sylvia received a letter from editor Margot Macdonald, who had been writing notes of encouragement on previous rejections, that the national magazine *Seventeen* was going to publish her short story "And Summer Will Not Come Again" after holding on to it for several months.

There is no doubt that Sylvia graduated from Bradford High School as one of the bright young stars of the community in 1950. Certainly, this elder child of an educated but not wealthy widow, a girl who had worked so hard to achieve her goals, had the best wishes and good will of her family and town as she prepared to head off to college. With that in mind, perhaps it is not difficult to imagine the townspeople's shock when only three years later, they read in the *Boston Herald* that this star was found after a massive search with a scratched face and wearing dungarees, slippers, and a green jersey, lying in the fetal position in a crawl space underneath her mother's house at 26 Elmwood Road. Despite her brilliant but disturbed mind's efforts at ending her life with an overdose of sleeping pills, her body fought back hard and hung on.

NOTES

1. Qtd. in Paul Alexander, *Rough Magic: A Biography of Sylvia Plath* (New York: Viking Press, 1991), p. 32.

2. Qtd. in Alexander, *Rough Magic*, p. 36.

3. Qtd. in Alexander, *Rough Magic*, p. 38.

4. Shakespeare, *The Tempest*, I:ii:397–401. *The Riverside Shakespeare*, 2nd ed. (Boston: Houghton Mifflin, 1997), p. 1667.

5. Qtd. in Alexander, *Rough Magic*, p. 51.

6. Qtd. in Alexander, *Rough Magic*, p. 59.

Chapter 4

THE ACADEMIC LIFE
(1950–1955)

SMITH COLLEGE

Sylvia's years as a student at Smith College from 1950 to 1955 have become legendary. It was true that she was beginning to publish poems and stories regularly in national magazines as she entered and continued through college. These publications gave her notoriety on campus even as she went to classes with all the other undergraduates. It was the later publications of her journals, however, that begin with the summer before her freshman year that give a meticulous accounting of college life for smart young women of the 1950s. Those years are made particularly vivid for thousands of readers who have never stepped foot on Smith's campus. Perhaps most notable of all during her Smith student years was the tragedy that took place in the summer between her junior and senior years and delayed her graduation by a year, a tragedy that she guardedly fictionalized in a novel less than a decade later and published under a pseudonym, *The Bell Jar*, by Victoria Lucas.

Founded in 1871 by Sophia Smith, who bequeathed $400,000 in a trust to establish an institution of higher learning for women, Smith College by the 1950s was regarded as one of the best institutions of higher learning for women in the United States. Enrollment at that time was about 2,400, and though admissions requirements were tough, and only bright women were enrolled, their hopes for after graduation were still fenced in by a society that expected their eventual fate would be marriage, family, home, and children at the sacrifice of a career. Any profession the women went into before those events occurred would take a backseat to their more important obligations in traditionally female roles once they entered into marriage. Consequently, not only were high grades and involvement in activities expected while at Smith, but dating different young men and analyzing compatibility and a prospective husband's prospects for a career became almost an unspoken part of the curriculum.

Even though seeking a mate was thought to be a natural part of college life, Smith, like most of the Seven Sisters colleges in New England, ran under a conservative set of rules. Students had curfews each night—10 P.M. Monday through Thursday; midnight on Fridays; and 1 A.M. on Saturdays. Students reported to chapel every Wednesday morning. Dinner each evening was formal, requiring students to dress up before they sat down to tables covered with candles and linen tablecloths. Men were not allowed in the dorms above the first floor, and if one should happen to go upstairs, the women on the floor were to shout "Man on floor" as a warning to all the others. Most women accepted these and other rules without question.

For its part, by 1950 the small community of Northampton existed primarily as a college town. Clustered near Amherst and South Hadley, it partnered with Amherst College and Mount Holyoke in various activities and resources, even as it does today. The red brick buildings of Smith sit in the middle of the town; perhaps the most distinctive physical feature of the campus at Plath's time was a pond called Paradise Pond that is still there. When Sylvia first arrived on campus, she moved into Haven House where she spent her freshman and sophomore years; she lived in Lawrence House for her junior and senior years.

Freshman year was marked by classes and publications as Sylvia adjusted to her new life at college. She had worked hard the previous summer. On August 11, "Bitter Strawberries," her first nationally published poem, appeared in The Christian Science Monitor, and on September 12, a short story, "Rewards of a New England Summer," appeared in the same publication. The story was based on her summer job before college—she had worked long hours six days a week for 10 weeks at Lookout Farm with migrant workers in order to earn a higher wage than normal student part-time jobs offered. The job required that she rise at six, bicycle five miles to the farm, work all day, then bicycle the five miles home. Her tasks included harvesting beans and radishes, weeding corn, setting out strawberry runners, and occasionally staffing the produce stand. The story speaks of her pride in the hard work; the narrator can almost see her reflection in the sheen of the eggplants on sale at the stand.

One evening in July 1950, after setting strawberry runners in the hot sun all day, she sat down in the empty house in Wellesley with a glass of milk and a shallow dish of blueberries and cream and opened a large, new notebook that would be the beginning of her famous published journals decades later. "I may never be happy," she wrote as the first sentence of her first entry, "but tonight I am content."[1] No wonder after such a summer of hard physical labor that the studious poet found the gracious buildings, living, and landscaping of Smith College a taste of paradise.

She took the new journal notebook with her to Smith and in it she related and mused about her arrival in Northampton and the changes in her surroundings. That fall, she took English, Introduction to French Literature, Botany, Art, European History, and gym. She found European History the most challenging of her classes. As a scholarship student, she needed to maintain at least a B overall average, or she risked dismissal. Her struggles in European History made her fearful enough that she might fall below this that she began working harder than ever to maintain her academic standing. The workload, made all the harder by the way she pushed herself, along with corresponding with her mother and others while faithfully writing in her journal and trying to write creatively as well (though finding less time for that those first weeks), forced her into depression and homesickness as early as mid-October. By November, she had another publication in *Seventeen*, a Keats-inspired poem called "Ode to a Bitten Plum." In the poem, the speaker considers a plum, thinking about the seeds as metaphors for abstractions like time and eternity.

Sylvia struck her classmates in Haven House as an ambitious loner.[2] She stood a good head above them and was approachable with a wide, ready smile lined in red lipstick; she had an attractive, rather than pretty, physical appearance. She was frequently alone, however, and did not seem interested in getting to know the other women on her floor or in her classes. Perhaps as a consequence of being there on scholarship, Sylvia appeared to the other students to be highly competitive. She did not like to share the limelight in terms of recognition or prizes; she wanted to win them for herself.

That October Sylvia learned who had given her the scholarship to attend Smith. She was popular writer Olive Higgins Prouty, whose best-known work was *Now, Voyager*, a novel that had been made into a film starring Bette Davis, and *Stella Dallas*, which had been made into a popular radio show as well as a film starring Barbara Stanwyck. That fall Sylvia wrote Ms. Prouty a letter of gratitude for her gift that moved the author to tears. In it, she described her influences as a writer, whom she claimed then to be Edna St. Vincent Millay, Stephen Vincent Benét, Virginia Woolf, and Sinclair Lewis. She also expressed her love of the Smith campus, the way the houses lit up at night, the view she had of Paradise Pond from her room, and the chimes. Upon receiving the letter, Olive Prouty invited her grateful scholarship recipient to her home in Brookline, Massachusetts, for tea over Christmas break. Sylvia could hardly wait for the semester to be over so that she could finally meet her author benefactor.

Olive Higgins Prouty lived in a mansion at 393 Walnut Street. Over tea and cucumber sandwiches, she and Sylvia discussed Smith and came around to their other mutual interest—writing. Sylvia expressed the desire to want to write about large subjects, to travel and have exotic adventures, but she was troubled because she had not experienced anything on that scale to write about as yet. Ms. Prouty asked her whether she had ever lived through any painful experiences or had any problems that seemed of vital importance when she was going through them. When Sylvia admitted that she had, Prouty advised her to write about those times. Through her actual life experiences, she advised the young author, she had all the material she would ever need.

While Sylvia was home at Wellesley for the remainder of her break, she learned her grades for the fall semester—English, B+; Gym, B-; Art, A; Botany, A; French, A-; and an A- in European History. She had no reason to fear losing her scholarship from Ms. Prouty. In fact, the popular author would go on to help Plath in many more ways than she could ever have expected.

Soon after she returned to Northampton for the spring semester, *Seventeen* notified her that her short story, "Den of Lions," had earned third place in its fiction contest and would be published in May 1951. By now, Sylvia had been corresponding with a young man named Eddie Cohen for several months. Eddie was a college English major from Chicago who wrote her first "fan letter" in early August 1950. The letter was in response to her short story, "And Summer Will Not Come Again" in *Seventeen*. Of "Den of Lions" Eddie wrote, "You are good, Syl—mighty good. You have the eyes and ears of a great writer. Personally, though, I wonder whether you have the heart of one."[3] That the letter bothered her may suggest that its message struck a nerve.

Sylvia's spring semester grades were: English, B+; French, A; Botany, A; Art, A; European History, A-; and Gym, C. She celebrated her first summer between years at college by taking a babysitting job with Dr. and Mrs. Frederick Mayo of 144 Beach Bluff Avenue in Swampscott, Massachusetts. Since her days with her maternal grandparents on Point Shirley, Sylvia had loved the beach and the sun. Taking care of the Mayo children and enjoying the beach seemed like the perfect solution to earning money while tanning and reading in her spare time. While the Mayo house was grand and located right on the beach, she soon found that the spare time she had hoped for after caring for the Mayo's three children was slim. That summer, however, she did read a novel that would make a deep impression on her later work, J. D. Salinger's *Catcher in the Rye*. Many readers point to similarities between this coming-of-age narrative of a troubled protagonist and Plath's *The Bell Jar*.

Sylvia had another taste of luxury when she first returned to Smith for her sophomore year and was invited, with all of Haven House, to the coming-out party of Maureen Buckley, sister of William F. Buckley. William had just published *God and Man at Yale*, and the Buckleys then, as now, were a wealthy family. The party was held at The Elms, the Buckley estate in Sharon, Connecticut. After being driven in cars the family provided to Stone House, the guest house near The Elms, the Haven House "Smithies" were chauffeured to the Sharon Inn for dinner by limousine. After dinner, Maureen's friends were returned to the Buckley mansion for dancing. The next day, after brunch, Sylvia's group of Smithies was driven back to Haven House in a black Cadillac. Immediately on returning, Sylvia wrote to her hard-working mother, Aurelia, about this extravagant night. Later, Aurelia admitted to enjoying living adventures such as these vicariously through her daughter.

In her sophomore year, Sylvia took Nineteenth and Twentieth Century Literature, Introduction to Politics, Writing, Visual Expression, Introduction to Religion, and Gym. At the same time, she had an ongoing relationship with Dick Norton, a young man she knew from Wellesley who had attended Yale and was now in medical school at Harvard. She continued to date other men as well. The chronic sinusitis the young poet had suffered from all her life and that contributed to Aurelia's decision to move from Winthrop inland to Wellesley hit her with a vengeance that fall. It forced Sylvia to check into the infirmary. Though her recovery was swift, she wrote at this time, "Sinusitis plunges me in manic depression."[4]

Soon after she left the infirmary, she had an interview with *Mademoiselle* about the College Board, a group of college writers from around the country who served a similar role to national correspondents for the magazine. Her schoolwork, emotional rollercoasters with various men, and outside writing work began to bear down on her stamina. Soon, she was drawing gravestones in her letters out of anxiety about upcoming writing assignments. Under one of these she wrote, "Life was fun while it lasted."[5] The work kept coming. To earn more money than her stories and poems were already bringing in, she began to report for the Press Board, a press pool of student journalists who wrote about Smith activities for local papers. Fall semester grades were: English, A (her first A in English at Smith); Writing, A; Religion, A-; Art, B; and Gym, B. Despite her grades, Sylvia began fretting over her writing talent when a story was rejected at

Seventeen. Concerns over men, sexual desire, and the double standard tormented and scrambled her thoughts and journal entries.

Much of her journals of the Smith years are filled with meditations and frustrations over society seemingly allowing men to be sexually active in the 1950s without ruining their reputations while females were expected to suppress their feelings and remain pure for their future husbands. Fear of pregnancy and a bad reputation for women kept the playing field uneven in the 1950s, and no one spoke of this with more anguish and anger than Sylvia Plath in her private journals. She would be a great writer, she wrote, if she did not have to face the choice of working at a high level against having a husband and family. The different ambitions of mind, heart, and body came at odds with one another, and she outwardly tried to reason how a talented woman could do important work with or without a husband and a family. The journal entries of her time at Smith did much to fuel Plath as a champion and martyr for feminists who read them three decades later.

In March, *Seventeen* notified her that her short story, "The Perfect Setup" had won an honorable mention in their annual fiction contest. Her other activities included teaching children's art classes at Northampton's People Institute, serving on Haven's House Committee, and chairing the Sophomore Prom Entertainment Committee. That the poet managed to write work publishable for national periodicals—an uncommon feat for someone her age in the 1950s or now—at the same time as she received high grades at Smith and participated in activities with an active dating life to go with it is testament to the high gear and perfectionist drive her life had spun into by the end of her sophomore year. After spring break, she wrote the story "Sunday at the Mintons" and almost on a whim sent it off to *Mademoiselle*. She earned $10 per month writing for the Springfield *Daily News*. Her awards that spring included induction into the arts honorary society, Alpha Phi Kappa, becoming a member of the Sophomore Push Committee—a designation of "special" girls in her class—and an invitation to join *The Smith Review* editorial board. By May, she had also received an invitation for a summer waitressing job at The Belmont hotel in West Harwick-by-the-Sea, Massachusetts.

Rather than waitress in the main dining room where tips would have made the summer job more lucrative, Sylvia found out when she arrived at The Belmont that her lack of waitressing experience placed her in the Side Hall, where employees ate and tips were much lower. She worked there for several weeks, picking up extra cash by setting linen out each evening after the main dining room had closed. During her time there, she received a telegram forwarded by her mother notifying her that she had won the *Mademoiselle* fiction contest for "Sunday at the Mintons." Armed with this important literary success, she tried to stick out the less-than-perfect summer job situation. It was clear by this time that Sylvia was hoping to make writing a profession that would help pay her bills.

Sinusitis struck Sylvia again while the position at The Belmont was still not producing the money she thought she needed to make for the summer. She returned to Wellesley, and her mother agreed that she should quit when she did not recover in time to return to The Belmont when they called. Instead, she decided to take a job as a mother's helper for Margaret Cantor at 276 Dorset Road in Chatham, Massachusetts. The job began on July 19, 1952. Cape Cod, with its beaches and sun, was just what she needed to regain her strength and vitality for another upcoming, grueling school year. About this time, Sylvia received a letter from Harold Strauss, editor-in-chief of Alfred A. Knopf publishers. He had just seen the proofs for "Sunday at the Mintons" that *Mademoiselle* managing editor Cyrilly Abels had sent over. He urged Sylvia to write a novel and send it to him. Sylvia was flattered and wrote back that she would consider his offer.

With a full-time writing career nearly in her grasp (four paid acceptances of poems and stories within three months), the fiction award in her pocket, and school work abated for the time being, Plath enjoyed her summer job at the Cantors' on the Cape. Neither she nor the family wanted her to leave at the end of August. Citing images from a poem she copied over at the front of her journal notebook, "Aubade" by Louis Macneice, she wrote in its pages on August 31, 1952:

> Oh, I bite, I bite on life like a sharp apple. Playing it like a fish, I am happy. And what is happy? It is a going always on. There is something better to be done than I have done, and spurred by the fair delusion of progress, I will seek to progress, to whip myself on, to more and more—to learning. Always. I have a well, deep, clear, and tartly sweet of living.... And I am nowhere near the ending.[6]

Sylvia, Warren, and Aurelia vacationed on the Cape after her job was over, and she spent some time visiting with Mr. Crockett in his backyard in Wellesley on September 20. While talking with her old high school mentor, Sylvia realized for the first time that she wanted to attend graduate school after Smith—preferably at Oxford or Cambridge, and she set achieving acceptance into one or the other as another new goal. She would try to finance the effort by applying for a Fulbright Scholarship.

News of her fiction prize was all over Smith when she returned as a junior that fall. Besides the appearance of "Sunday at the Mintons," a poem,

"White Phlox," had also appeared in *The Christian Science Monitor*. If attention as a nationally published and recognized writer had not been duly paid to her before, the fall of her junior year her profile on campus rose significantly. She moved into Lawrence House, a "self-help" house that offered the equivalent of work-study hours for its inhabitants. Despite her growing national profile as a writer, Sylvia waited tables and performed other household tasks as a member of the house.

Rather than remain boosted by her summer successes, back at Smith, Sylvia sunk into growing depression over fears of not measuring up. It seemed as more publications came, she grew less and less confident in her abilities. Still, these feelings did not deter her from continuing to submit her work to magazines and competitions. In October, *Seventeen* published her story, "The Perfect Set-up" and awarded another story, "Initiation," second prize in its fiction contest. These successes fueled Sylvia's most pressing goal that fall—to win a guest editorship at *Mademoiselle* through the College Board.

The application process for the guest editorship was arduous and time-consuming. While straining to keep at the top of her class in all of her subjects, Sylvia had much extra writing to do to fill out the applications. The first task was to write a 1,500-word critique of the latest August college issue of the magazine, including an overview of the entire magazine, then a focus on the section of it that interested her most. Out of 2,000 applicants for a College Board slot, 750 were accepted. One had to be a member of the College Board (student correspondent positions) first to apply further toward the guest editorship, of which there were only 20 open slots. Sylvia made the first cut. That meant that during the school year she had to write three assignments as a correspondent with the College Board. Each assignment was eligible for one of 10 prizes, 1 $50 and 9 $10 prizes. Over the three assignments, this created a pool of 30 top assignment writers from which the 20 guest editors were chosen.

While she was going through the application process that meant so much to her, Dick Norton became ill, and tuberculosis was feared. Because of her contact with him, Sylvia had to undergo a chest x-ray to be cleared. While Dick was given long-term hospital care at the Ray Brook Sanitarium in Saranac, New York, she wrote to him with curious messages of envy. He could rest and read and be idle, she lamented, while she was drowning in work.

Danger signals began emanating from her in several directions—in her letters to Dick, in conversations with her former roommate Marcia Brown, and in letters home to Aurelia. She began having episodes of crying uncontrollably and writing fearful letters in which she wrote that she was contemplating suicide. She wrote in her journal, "You have lost all delight in life. . . . You want to go home, back to the womb."[7] The focus became her physical science class. If she only did not have to take this class that writers would never need anyhow, things would be better.

A trip home for Thanksgiving helped a little with a visit to the Cantors. *Seventeen* published her poem "Twelfth Night" in December, but at the same time she endured her second rejection from *The New Yorker*. She had tried them again after her first form rejection letter came back with a "Try us again" scribbled anonymously at the bottom; this time their rejection of two villanelles included penciled comments on the poems. Insomnia and a sore throat kicked in, and that seemed to be the last straw before Sylvia sought help for herself. After seeing the Smith College psychiatrist for her crying spells, she checked herself into the infirmary until Christmas break.

Over semester break, she visited Dick in Saranac. There was a ski slope nearby, and his father suggested that they go skiing; it would do Dick good, he said. Sylvia was a novice, and Dick was not much better. While skiing with Dick giving her instructions, she fell and fractured her fibula, a break that required her entire leg be put in a cast.

By the time she went back to Smith in January to maneuver around the campus on crutches, Sylvia heard that her petition to audit her spring chemistry class had been approved by the board. This meant that she had convinced them to allow her to sit in on the classes to gain knowledge about science, but she did not have to take tests, do labs, or complete the reading. That a college would grant such a request to an undergraduate is highly unusual and is testament to Sylvia's professional writing profile by this time and her powers of persuasion on her own behalf. Her chemistry class alleviated, that left a seminar in Milton and classes in Modern Poetry, Creative Writing, and Honors hours for the spring 1953 semester. When her grades for the fall arrived, she received an A- in her dreaded Physics class after all, an A- in Creative Writing, and the only A out of 10 students in Medieval Literature. When her cast was removed in late February, Sylvia felt another surge of energy to keep working hard.

That spring, even as she audited Chemistry, attended her other classes, and wrote and worked on her *Mademoiselle* application assignments (she sent in an extra short story to them, for good measure, but it was later returned), Sylvia's writing continued to be published in national magazines and her literary career grew. *Seventeen* accepted "Sonnet: To a Dissembling Spring" and published "Carnival Nocturne." *Harper's* accepted the two villanelles that *The New Yorker* had rejected: "Doomsday" and "To Eva Descending the Stair," as well as "Go Get the Goodly Squab." *The*

Smith Review appointed Sylvia editor-in-chief for her senior year. British poet W.H. Auden, was a visiting professor that semester at Smith, and when Sylvia heard him read, she proclaimed that she had found her God. She wrote this comment in the front of her copy of his collected poems. Auden's eccentric appearance around Smith's campus, sporting unkempt hair and bedroom slippers and quite often intoxicated, only fueled her awe about the quality of his poetry.

At the end of April, Sylvia received the telegram from Marybeth Little at *Mademoiselle* that she had worked and hoped for since the previous summer—she had won a guest editorship at the magazine and was to report in New York City on June 1 and be available to work through June 26. The pay for this period was $150, a fraction of the sum Sylvia normally needed to make over the summer to cover expenses. However, the opportunity was too good to pass up, and Sylvia devised a plan of how to make up the difference. This summer she would trust that her writing would earn the money she needed.

She signed up for Harvard Summer School's fiction-writing class that would start after the editorship in July. It was being taught by Frank O'Connor, and Sylvia was reasonably confident she would get in and hopeful that she could sell the story she would write in that workshop. She sent in the prize-winning story, "Sunday at the Mintons" as her writing sample for the Harvard application. Her other plan was to sell a more slick work of fiction, "I Lied for Love," to *True Story*. The pulp story was not her normal genre, but she wrote it quickly simply to sell for what she hoped would be easy cash.

With the upcoming editorship beginning June 1, the end of her junior year was even more pressured than usual. She had to take her final exams early to be done in time to go to New York, plus *Mademoiselle* had given her assignments that she needed to begin right away, even before she arrived in the city. Good grades and prizes again ushered in the end of the school year and the beginning of summer—Modern Poetry, A; Creative Writing, A; Milton, B+. She was now at the top of the Smith class of 1954. One wonders where her standing would have been had she not been allowed to audit Chemistry, though her A- in Physics the semester before indicates she would have likely remained in the top spot. Smith awarded her two prestigious poetry awards that spring as well—the Elizabeth Babcock Poetry Prize and the Ethel Olin Corbin Prize. The *Daily Hampshire Gazette* ran an article praising their local student reporter's garnering of the *Mademoiselle* guest editorship. After two days home in Wellesley to pack and write up her early assignment of an interview with poet Elizabeth Bowen, Sylvia was on a train headed for New York. Unfortunately, the old adage, "be careful what you wish for" would become entirely fitting for Sylvia's summer of '53.

MADEMOISELLE GUEST EDITORSHIP

Readers of Plath's 1963 novel, *The Bell Jar*, say that it is an autobiographical narrative depicting the poet's experience in New York City working as a guest editor for *Mademoiselle* and the aftermath of this experience, and this is, for the most part, correct. The guises of fiction are so thin in the novel, in fact, that it was not published in the United States for nearly 10 years after its first appearance in England for fear of libel suits and also to honor Aurelia Plath's wishes. The novel was just too close to home. Sylvia and the 19 other guest editors stayed at the Barbizon Hotel, for example, thinly disguised as the Amazon Hotel in the novel. Her supervisor, the managing editor of *Mademoiselle*, was named Cyrilly Abels, not Jay Cee as in the fictional account. Mrs. Plath's concerns over hurting living persons' feelings in America were the novel to be published there are dramatized in Sylvia's naming the character modeled after her benefactor, Olive Higgins Prouty, Philomena Guinea. In the novel, Ms. Guinea's popular novels that made her millions of dollars are described in less-than-flattering terms.

Sylvia had already established her pattern of writing what she knew from her own personal experience, as she was advised in December 1950 by Ms. Prouty herself, so doing so for her first novel probably comes as no surprise. That said, one should not read the novel in place of a biographical account of the events that happened that summer and believe that they are one-for-one identical. Characters blend from composites of real people and episodes are sometimes exaggerated or otherwise manipulated for dramatic effect. Years later, Mrs. Plath argued that Sylvia wrote the fictionalized account of that summer as a "potboiler" to make money, and that the ingratitude that the protagonist appears to feel toward her loved ones and benefactors was not a true depiction of Sylvia's own feelings toward their real-life models.

The other 19 guest editors at *Mademoiselle* that year were: Ruth L. Abramson from the University of Pennsylvania; Margaret Affleck, Brigham Young University; Nedra Anderwert, Washington University; Candy Bolster, Bryn Mawr; Betty-Jo Boyle, Allegany College; Anne Burnside, University of Maryland; Malinda Edgington, Miami University; Laurie Glazer, University of Michigan; Gloria Kirshner, Barnard College; Dinny Lain, Stephens College; Carol LeVarn, Sweet Briar; Grace Macleod, University of Oklahoma; Madelyn Mathers, University of

Washington; Eileen McLaughlin, Pratt Institute; Neva Nelson, San Jose State University; Del Schmidt, Skidmore College; Anne Shawber, Northwestern University; Laurie Totten, Syracuse University; and Janet Wagner from Knox College. Each woman was assigned a different editing task for the forthcoming August 1953 college issue under the guardianship and supervision of the corresponding professional editor at the magazine. The tasks ran the gamut from fashion to fiction, from health and beauty editor to managing editor.

In four short weeks, the women had much work to do on a steep learning curve. They were, after all, actually putting together a magazine for national circulation by the time they met all of their deadlines. The professional editors seemed intent on making sure the young women felt the responsibility of the task; they mentored them, but there is little sign that they were prepared to cover for them if any of the college students failed in her duties. The pressure the young women felt, many of them visiting the large city of New York for the first time as well, was enormous.

Besides the high workload and level of responsibility, the entire experience was another marketing scheme on the part of the magazine to increase sales and advertising. What the guest editors wore, what social functions they attended, the publicity they generated when appearing as a group or individually at various venues in town—all of these factors played into the profits the magazine hoped to achieve with their annual college issues. Consequently, not only were the guest editors' days filled with interviews, writing, reading, meetings, and other normal editorial work, but their lunch hours, evenings, and weekends were completely scheduled for them with social functions they were expected to dress for and participate in with enthusiasm. For many of the college women, some coming from small towns and rural areas around the country, and all coming from the relative quiet of 1950s college campuses, the whirlwind of city life became intoxicating. The stimulation overloaded many of them, and it did not take long before they caught on to the fact that they were expected to be as much runway models put on display for advertising purposes as actual working journalists. Some responded to the artificiality of the experience in more healthy ways than others.

By 1953, New York City had come through World War II as a boomtown. The establishment of the United Nations headquarters in lower Manhattan after the war ensured that the city had global importance and influence. New skyscrapers of steel and glass shot up between the older ones of stone. Tourists flocked to the city in record numbers, and artists began settling in the various neighborhoods—intellectuals and writers moved into low-rent housing near Columbia University on the city's

Upper West Side. Greenwich Village attracted sculptors and painters such as abstract expressionists Jackson Pollack, Willem de Kooning, and Barnett Newman, who would later be part of a movement called the New York School of art. George Balanchine choreographed dances in this period, and Joe DiMaggio amazed baseball fans with his talents in game after game at Yankee Stadium in the Bronx.

The hot news event around town when the 20 college women arrived that June was the pending execution of the Rosenbergs, which was to take place within the month. In March 1951, Julius and Ethel Rosenberg had been convicted as Russian spies and were sentenced to the electric chair at Sing Sing prison in New York. Appeals over the intervening two years did nothing to overturn the ruling, and President Eisenhower refused to grant clemency. When the young guest editors walked by newsstands on their way into the Barbizon Hotel where they all stayed on *Mademoiselle*'s tab, the front pages that looked back at them were filled with stories about the Rosenbergs. The Rosenbergs were civilians, not government employees, who were caught up in the 1950s anti-Communist paranoia of the McCarthy era. Senator Joseph McCarthy led hearings where a simple accusation of being a Communist "black-balled" a person into trouble and often brought them before McCarthy's commission to answer questions. Many political activists who spoke out against government policies and other thinkers such as artists and writers were brought before the government and questioned as though they must be Communist spies.

The Rosenbergs' plight bothered Sylvia immensely, and she became emotionally involved with the drama of their story from the moment she arrived in the city, carefully watching her watch and carrying their expected death date and hour in her mind. Though their situation is complex (some believe Julius did tell important secrets to the Russians but his wife did not; others believe both were innocent), their case was one of the highest, if not the highest, profiled case of the McCarthy era.

Sylvia's first week at the magazine began Monday, June 1, 1953, with a general meeting of the guest editors at 9:00 A.M. at *Mademoiselle*'s offices at 575 Madison Avenue. Betsy Talbot Blackwell, editor-in-chief, welcomed the women and spoke about the magazine's expectations for their internships. She introduced the other professional editors to the women, two of whom had reputations in the business for working with well-known writers. Fiction editor Margarita G. Smith was the sister of Carson McCullers and was known for publishing the first work of Truman Capote and others. As the winner of the fiction contest, Sylvia had expected to be guest fiction editor, but she was not given that assignment. Instead, she worked for managing editor Cyrilly Abels, another famous editor who knew writers such as Dylan Thomas and Katherine Anne Porter.

At 10:00 A.M., the women separated to the offices of their respective supervising editors for individual meetings. They also posed for individual photographs, which seemed to trouble some of the young editors right away. Both Sylvia, who was asked to sit and hold a rose, and another guest editor shed tears over the photo shoot out of confusion and embarrassment. The photographer was frustrated, saying he was used to working with only the top models.

As guest managing editor, Sylvia had responsibility over more parts of the magazine than any of the other editors. She also had more writing assignments. It did not help her awkward feelings that first morning when Cyrilly Abels told her that she had to rewrite her "Poets on Campus" piece to fit in better with Mademoiselle's style. She worked at this task at a typewriter table all that morning beside Abels's full-size desk. Her work that first week included finishing her revision, writing "Mlle's Last Word," reading manuscripts, and typing rejection letters. Given her own form letter rejections received from The New Yorker, it must have given her some measure of special interest to send a rejection letter for work submitted by a member of its staff. The experience of seeing firsthand the inner workings of a national magazine was invaluable to her future career. Outside the office, she attended a fashion show at the Hotel Roosevelt and took a tour of Richard Hudnut's Fifth Avenue salon.

Her work the second week of the month included meeting Paul Engle, founder of the Iowa Writer's Workshop and editor of that year's O. Henry short story contest. She also met Vance Bourjaily, a first-time novelist and editor of the premier issue of the literary magazine Discovery. The magazine took all of the women to a formal dance at the St. Regis Hotel Terrace Room, where there were two bands so the music never stopped playing and all of the tablecloths and decorations were pink. Another night that week, the guest editors were treated to a performance of the New York City Ballet, which included such dances as George Balanchine's Metamorphoses and Scotch Symphony, Lew Christensen's Con Amore, and Jerome Robbins's Fanfare. On the way there, the taxi Sylvia was riding in became caught in traffic. Disc jockey Art Ford approached the car full of young women and began flirting with them until Sylvia and Carol LeVarn promised to meet him at 3:00 in the morning after he went off the air. After the ballet, she and Carol went to the bars along Third Avenue and met Art Ford, who took them to Greenwich Village for early morning hours of sexually charged dancing between Ford and LeVarn.

Sylvia arrived at work exhausted from no sleep. Coming straight to New York from her junior year at college and the pressures of the application process, along with needing to begin her assignments early and having heavy responsibilities at the magazine were finally beginning to take their toll. Added to the work pressures were all the social obligations expected of the guest editors. Partying into the wee hours of the morning on top of all that was more than the perfectionist intern, and her body, could physically and emotionally handle. Soon she began complaining about the more menial details of the job; one late afternoon, a full-time editor found her crying at her desk over having to work late.

Over the weekend of June 13, Warren Plath graduated from Exeter, but his sister was not there to celebrate with him and their mother, and the event is not even noted on the busy calendar she kept at the time. Aurelia's younger child had fared as well as her eldest had in school. Warren was accepted on a full scholarship to Harvard, which he planned to begin in the fall. Sylvia wrote her mother and Warren a letter, saying that she did not have the train fare to go to Andover, but that her thoughts would be with them both all weekend. Meanwhile, she spent at least some of the time that weekend preparing and sending in her late application to Harvard's Summer School.

Week three of the guest editorship was the most notable of the four for the poet for several reasons. On Monday, the editors toured *Living* magazine, and on Tuesday they visited the advertising offices of Batton, Barton, Durstine, and Osborn. They were given a luncheon by the ad agency that included a crabmeat salad that Sylvia's always voracious appetite enjoyed fully with several helpings. Tuesday evening, Sylvia went on a date with Gary Kaminloff, a young man from Wellesley who was working at the United Nations as a simultaneous interpreter. Following her date, she became ill in her room at the Barbizon and headed for the rest room. There, she found several other guest editors all sick. It was determined that the crabmeat salad they had all had for lunch was contaminated, and they were all suffering from ptomaine poisoning. Few of them made it into work the next morning.

The pressure to perform continued that week, food poisoning or not, and the young women were expected to return to their respective *Mademoiselle* offices one by one as soon as they possibly could. Later that week, most attended the various functions that had been planned for them aside from their normal duties. These included touring the United Nations and magazine offices of *Vanity Fair* and *Charm*, visiting John Fredericks Hats, and attending the premiere of the film, *Let's Do It Again*, starring Jane Wyman and Ray Milland.

The long-anticipated execution of the Rosenbergs took place on Friday, June 19. Sylvia began that day in protest of the event. Thinking the execution was occurring that morning at 9:00 A.M., she refused to eat breakfast, challenging her comrades at the table with the indignity of enjoying a hotel breakfast of fried eggs as innocent people were being fried not far away along the Hudson River. Fellow guest editor Janet Wagner later recalled Sylvia looking at her watch at precisely 9 A.M. and saying that the execution was happening right at that exact moment (actually it did not occur until later that evening). Janet recalled seeing welts rising up all along Sylvia's arms, which she held out for Janet to see. Though they never spoke of it then or afterwards, Wagner remembered the eerie occurrence for the rest of her life.

Some of the other guest editors recalled other incidents of odd behavior during their internship with Sylvia. One, later called the "Dylan Thomas episode," involved Abels taking Candy Bolster, the guest fiction editor, to meet Welsh poet Dylan Thomas, when Sylvia was out of the office. Abels had been negotiating with Thomas over the rights to his drama *Under Milkwood*. When Sylvia found out that she had missed the opportunity to meet the poet, she became furious and tried for two days afterwards, according to other guest editors' accounts, to force a chance meeting with him on her own. She loitered in the hallway around his hotel room door and outside a tavern he frequented, but she never saw him. Given her later notoriety primarily as a poet, the severity of her disappointment at missing him is perhaps understandable; however, the drama and effort that she put into trying to meet him after the opportunity had already passed struck her fellow editors as extreme.

That weekend, the guest editors attended a New York Yankees–Detroit Tigers baseball game at Yankee Stadium, and some of them also went to a dance at the Forest Hills tennis club in Queens. At the dance, Sylvia had to fight off a vigorous sexual advance by the United Nations delegate from Peru. Thankfully, the date *Mademoiselle* had provided for her took her and Janet Wagner back to the hotel.

The last week of the four-week internship was another busy one, but all the women knew they were headed for the finish line in terms of deadlines and their responsibilities. That week, they toured the offices of the New York *Herald Tribune* and visited Macy's Department Store. They also saw George Bernard Shaw's *Misalliance* at the Barrymore Theatre. Betsy Talbot Blackwell had a farewell cocktail party for them at her Fifth Avenue apartment. After the deadlines had all been met, and the August issue had been "put to bed," Cyrilly Abels took Sylvia out to lunch on her last day of work out of appreciation for her efforts. As the major contributor to the issue, Sylvia's work that appeared in the magazine included her interview with Elizabeth Bowen and "Poets on Campus"; "*Mlle's* Last Word"; captions and blurbs under pictures; and a poem, "Mad Girl's Love Song." She also modeled in two photographs—one taken from above with all the editors standing in the shape of a star at Central Park and one of her alone as a poet, sitting on the couch, holding a red rose. As one of the 20, she also had her palm read and interpreted for "Jobography," an article that predicted the futures of the talented and capable young women who had put together the issue.

Sylvia's personal copy of the August 1953 issue of *Mademoiselle* she helped publish is part of the Plath collection at Smith College. It is bound in a library hardcover binding with her name stamped on the front in gold. The magazine is inscribed to her with kind words by the editor-in-chief, Betsy Talbot Blackwell. Interestingly, the magazine's advertising images illustrate well the problem that Plath writes about so frequently in her journal—the dilemma smart women of the 1950s found themselves in fighting against wanting a career but having to succumb to social pressures to marry, have a family, and be subservient to men. On the pages opposite Sylvia's writing, for example, are ads for Ardmoor coats and suits and Monet moniker jewelry. The cover of the magazine shows a college co-ed modeling a tartan skirt. The dilemma is made even clearer in the copy Plath wrote for the magazine that was printed with the photo of the guest editors standing in a star formation:

> We're stargazers this season, bewitched by an atmosphere of evening blue. Foremost in the fashion constellation we spot *Mlle's* own tartan, the astronomic versatility of sweaters, and men, men, men—we've even taken the shirts off their backs! Focusing our telescope on college news around the globe, we debate and deliberate. Issues illuminated: academic freedom, the sorority controversy, our much labeled (and libeled) generation. From our favorite fields, stars of the finest magnitude shed a bright influence on our plans and jobs and futures. Although horoscopes for our ultimate orbits aren't yet in, we Guest Eds. are counting on a favorable forecast with this send-off from *Mlle.*, the star of the campus.[8]

1953 SUICIDE ATTEMPT

The disillusionment of the experience she had worked so hard to be able to have at *Mademoiselle* in New York tore at Sylvia's already weak-

ened emotional, physical, and mental state as the whirlwind month of
June 1953 came to an end. Janet Wagner later claimed that Sylvia came
to her room at the Barbizon the Saturday morning they were all checking
out and said she had thrown all of her clothing off the roof of the hotel in
protest of the false bill of goods they all had been sold. Sylvia, in a strange
kind of stupor, Janet claimed (Sylvia's mother later denied that it happened), asked to borrow Janet's green dirndl skirt and white peasant
blouse to wear home. In return, she insisted Janet take her bathrobe.

Getting off the train in Wellesley, Sylvia was delighted to see her
mother and Grammy Schober waiting for her. They talked in the car on
the way back to the house, catching up on each other's events. Sylvia was
obviously exhausted and looked forward to a few days off before heading
out to Cambridge to the fiction workshop with Frank O'Connor. They
had not even arrived back at the house, however, before Aurelia gave her
the bad news, stating it as carefully as she could—that Sylvia's application
to the fiction writing class at Harvard Summer School had been rejected.

Though she was used to sending out short stories and poems to magazines and receiving rejection letters for them, to be rejected for a college
class left Sylvia stunned. Academia had always been her strongest suit—
it had always come through for her in the past. Not only that, but she had
hoped to sell the story she would have written in the class to help meet
her expenses for her upcoming senior year at Smith. This upset on top of
the disillusionment she was feeling over her month in New York left her
feeling rudderless, like she was a failure in a new world that she did not
know how to negotiate. She began to doubt her talents again. When she
arrived home, she wrote a letter to Wilbury Crockett that struck him as
strange, apologizing to him for letting him down.

She decided she would not attend Harvard Summer School and take
any other classes, but that left her with the rest of the summer with no
plans or way to make money. She was unable to write or study. She attempted to read for her senior thesis, which at that time she thought
would be on James Joyce. A *Portrait of the Artist* in Plath's copy of *The
Portable James Joyce*, still in the archives, is heavily annotated. Even that
effort, however, failed her. She was losing sleep. Her mother offered to
teach her shorthand to take up her time, and their morning sessions are
noted on Sylvia's calendar. After only a handful of lessons, however,
Sylvia said the squiggles and swirls made her dizzy and she gave up.

For a short time, she had a part-time job as a nurse's aid at Newton-
Wellesley Hospital feeding patients who were too weak to feed themselves. Aurelia thought helping others would help snap Sylvia out of
thinking so much of herself and her own problems. She did not realize

that Sylvia was sinking into something deeper than a blue mood out of fatigue and disappointment. Sylvia was gravely ill.

In July, Sylvia was writing death wishes and thoughts in her journal. She was still having trouble sleeping. On one trip to the shore with friends, she flirted with dunking under the water and never coming up. She began thinking of suicide almost nonstop and what methods would be best. One day her mother noticed cuts partly healed on her daughter's legs. When she confronted her about them, Sylvia admitted to taking razor blades to them just to see if she had the nerve to use them to harm herself.

After this admission, Aurelia immediately sought help for her daughter with their family physician, Dr. Francesca Racioppi, who recommended a psychiatrist, Dr. J. Peter Thornton. After a few examinations by Dr. Thornton, Sylvia still refused to communicate with him or discuss her thoughts. At his recommendation, Aurelia reluctantly agreed to allow her daughter to undergo electroshock therapy on an outpatient basis to treat her for severe depression. Sylvia had her first treatment on Wednesday, July 29, 1953, marked in her calendar as "shockT."

Electroshock therapy was overused in the 1950s to treat psychiatric patients and when it was used, it was not used effectively or well. That first day set a routine of appointments in motion. Because she did not drive, Aurelia had a neighbor drive her and Sylvia to the Valley Head Hospital. The doctor had Aurelia and the neighbor sit outside in a waiting area, while Sylvia underwent the treatment. The treatment involved placing metal probes on the temples that shot strong currents of electricity charging through the patient's body. Once the treatment was complete, the doctor brought Sylvia out to the waiting area, where her mother and neighbor drove her home. Dr. Thornton treated Sylvia for the first few times, but then he went on vacation and left a Dr. Tillotson in charge of several more sessions.

Years later, on the rare occasions that this sort of treatment was deemed helpful for a patient, a muscle relaxant or general anesthetic was administered first. The theory was that the shocks lessened a patient's anxiety by interfering with the brain's capacity to remember and replay anxiety-causing thoughts. After the treatment, nurses and doctors stayed with the patient to monitor his or her recovery, thereby helping alleviate the patient's natural feelings of fear and abandonment. Because Sylvia was not given a relaxant before the treatment, her body was tense with fear, and she was likely almost electrocuted. When the nurses left her alone on the table afterwards, she experienced feelings of abandonment and vulnerability that no person ought to have to go through, especially a patient who is ill and incapacitated.

That Aurelia took Sylvia home and then had to leave her alone so often to keep working through the summer to pay the bills left Sylvia even more vulnerable to danger. As a side effect of the shock therapy, her restless, sleepless nights became more chronic, to the point of severe insomnia. In August, Sylvia did not sleep for weeks on end and began taking sleeping pills, which were having little to no effect. One week in her calendar is completely crossed out with a large black X dug into the paper. Another day in this period is marked in pencil, "Not here." Becoming more fearful over her daughter's continuing deterioration, Aurelia gave her two pills for the night and locked up the remaining 48 sleeping pills of a new bottle in a lockbox. She hid the key in her dresser drawer in the bedroom she shared again with her daughter since Warren was also home for the summer.

Eerily, Sylvia's calendar, so full of notations of classes, meetings, and New York City appointments for the year of 1953, goes blank after the last week in August. On Monday, August 24, 1953, at about 2:00 P.M., Sylvia waited for her mother to leave the house with a friend to watch a film of Queen Elizabeth II's coronation. Grammy and Grampy Schober, recently back home from a vacation on the Cape, were sitting in the backyard. Sylvia broke into the lockbox, retrieved the bottle of sleeping pills, and went out to the dining room. She placed a note against a bowl of flowers on the dining room table that read, "Have gone for a long walk. Will be home tomorrow."[9] In the kitchen, she poured herself a jar of water and took a blanket, the water, and the bottle of pills with her to the cellar.

There was a crawl space under the front porch that one could get to from a two-and-a-half-foot entrance in the wall of the cellar. The hole to the crawl space was five feet up from the floor and was covered by a stack of firewood. Sylvia removed the firewood from the top of the stack, placed the water, blanket, and pills inside the hole, heaved herself up into it, and replaced the wood in front of the hole. Then she lay down in the crawl space, wrapped the blanket around her, and started placing pills on her tongue, one at a time, followed by sips of water. She had not yet finished taking all the pills in the bottle when she slipped away, losing consciousness.

Just as she had experienced dread when Otto told her to go to the beach with the children over 20 years earlier, Aurelia could not stop feeling uneasy during the plotless movie of Queen Elizabeth II's coronation. While she made herself stay until the end, she asked her friend to drive her straight home. There, she found Sylvia's note. She explained the events of the last month to her parents, who had not yet known about them from being away on their vacation. When she did so, all three of them became concerned that Sylvia's note was not about a long walk at all. When her daughter did not return by 5:00 that evening, Aurelia called the police, and a public search began. By Tuesday morning, the search was on from 26 Elmwood Road top to bottom to Boston to everywhere around Wellesley. The radio put out a missing person bulletin, and the story of the missing successful Smith College senior hit the front page of the Boston *Globe* and also appeared in the Boston *Herald.* By Tuesday afternoon, the Associated Press put out updates about the search over the wires, and the news about Sylvia's disappearance appeared in several afternoon newspapers.

Nearly 100 volunteers joined the effort to search for Sylvia. These included neighbors, friends, Post 80 of the Explorer Scouts, and members of the American Legion. The Andover State Police had bloodhounds out sniffing for clues, but the rain that week may have hampered their efforts. By late Tuesday, Aurelia's fears turned even more severe when she discovered the lockbox of sleeping pills had been pried open and the new bottle full of pills was missing.

The Boston *Globe* continued to run the story on its front page on Wednesday, now with interviews of Aurelia and pictures of Sylvia and the whole family. Aurelia thought that the publicity might prompt Sylvia to report in, or help anyone who had seen her to contact police. She and the family regrouped over lunch about what to do, their concerns rising by the hour. At 12:45 P.M., Grammy Schober decided to go downstairs and put some laundry in, to at least keep the family going with their basic needs as a way to help. While she was at the washer, she heard a faint moaning behind the pile of firewood and immediately called for Warren.

Warren rushed downstairs and unpiled the logs away from the opening to the crawl space, as his grandmother asked. As soon as he did so, they saw Sylvia inside. She was wrapped in the blanket, barely awake, with a bleeding cut on her right cheek. She was covered in her own vomit, but she was alive.

Aurelia called the police and Officer Theodore McGlone came right away, since he was already in the neighborhood, searching garages for the missing girl. Sylvia was transported to Newton-Wellesley Hospital, the same hospital where she had worked a short time before. From the count of pills left in the bottle they found in the crawl space, eight, and the two Aurelia said she had given Sylvia as a normal dose out of the new bottle, the police and doctors concluded that the young writer had swallowed 40 pills in her effort to end her life. The pills made her vomit, and the vomiting expelled much of the drug out of her system, actually saving her. The cut was apparently a scrape from the cement when she had roused sometime during the ordeal enough to sit up and then had fallen over. Though the cut was not particularly severe, it had become infected, and she would wear the scar of it on her face for the rest of her life.

The evening editions of the *Globe* and other papers reported that she had been found. The wide press accounts had at least one good outcome—Olive Higgins Prouty had been vacationing at the Spruce Point Inn in Boothbay Harbor, Maine, when she ran across the story of Sylvia's disappearance. Calling the police department, she found out that Sylvia had since been found. She telegrammed Aurelia offering her concerns and, even more importantly, her help both emotionally and financially.

Sylvia's condition stabilized with penicillin injections fighting her infection and an around-the-clock nursing suicide watch for her psychiatric illness. On September 3, she was transferred to the psychiatric ward of the Massachusetts General Hospital. Olive Higgins Prouty arrived to offer not only long-distance support and financial backing, but also actual hands-on help to Aurelia with Sylvia's care. From then on, Aurelia counted Olive in on all consultations about what to do to help her daughter.

When it became clear that an indefinite but believed to be relatively short time in an institution was necessary for Sylvia's recovery, Olive wanted Sylvia to go to a private hospital where she and her husband had both been to previously for treatments—Silver Hill in New Canaan, Connecticut. The facility was almost country-club-like in appearance and its administrators had assured Olive that it would cover the expense of Sylvia's treatment from a foundation that Olive contributed to heavily, thus saving her money. The other option was McLean Hospital in Belmont, Massachusetts, a branch of Massachusetts General Hospital that also had a reputation for being one of the best in the country. Aurelia decided to go with McLean, but this choice against Olive's preference did not stop Ms. Prouty from footing the entire bill for Sylvia's treatment. She did so after negotiating with both the hospital and staff to reduce their fees based on the Plath's financial status.

After undergoing different treatment methods such as insulin injections, psychotherapy, and others, Sylvia met her new psychiatrist, Dr. Ruth Tiffany Barnhouse. Dr. Barnhouse would change Sylvia's life not only by helping her recover from her nervous breakdown, but also as a figure she could admire as a role model of an independent, professional woman. Dr. Barnhouse was related to the jewelry-store Tiffanys, and she had been educated at Barnard and Columbia Medical School. A divorced mother of two, Barnhouse was now married to a doctor named William Beuscher. Both her Ivy League background and her attitudes toward life as an independent woman helped bring Sylvia out of her shell to begin talk-ing about things that had been bothering her since she was child.

One day, during a breakthrough in her psychotherapy, Sylvia said that she hated her mother. Rather than be shocked or respond in some way that would deepen Sylvia's guilt over this admission, Dr. Barnhouse sim-ply replied, "I suppose you do."[10] The doctor also listened to Sylvia's com-plaints about the double standard of sexual activity for men versus women and had Sylvia fitted for a diaphragm birth control device. In a rare move for the 1950s, the doctor encouraged her to experiment with sex. Later into the treatment, Dr. Barnhouse had a long meeting with Aurelia and explained to her that, despite the bad experience with it that Sylvia had before, her team of doctors had determined that another dose of elec-troshock therapy was indicated.

From December 15 until Christmas, Dr. Barnhouse administered the treatments and watched Sylvia carefully. Almost immediately after these treatments, Sylvia began to recover. During the Christmas holidays, her depression seemed to disappear, and she was getting back to herself again. During one of her visits home to Wellesley from McLean during this pe-riod, Sylvia went to Harvard and out on a date with Philip McCurdy, an-other young man she knew from her hometown. She explained to Philip that she had tried to kill herself because she feared she had lost her talent. Whether it was true or not, she also told him she had tried to slit her throat once when she was ten. Philip could see a scar. They returned to Wellesley and dinner at Philip's house. When he drove Sylvia back to 26 Elmwood Road, Sylvia made sexual advances to Philip outside her mother's house in the front seat of the car. Surprised, Philip went along, and Sylvia, most likely as a result of Dr. Barnhouse's suggestion that she experiment, had her first complete sexual encounter.

By the end of January, Sylvia was released from McLean Hospital and was deemed ready to go back to Smith for the spring 1954 term. She would not be able to graduate with her class, and she would have a light-ened class load in view of her illness. Aurelia, thinking her daughter was better, resumed her normal habit of avoiding talking about difficult sub-jects, like Otto's death, unless she absolutely had to do so. The breakdown was behind them now, she thought, and they could begin again. On Sylvia's release from McLean, Aurelia heard from Otto's sister. She in-formed her that Otto's mother had been hospitalized once for depression, and a sister and a niece had also suffered from the same disease. Unfortu-nately, Aurelia told neither Sylvia nor her doctor this important informa-tion.

RETURN TO SMITH

Sylvia's workload at Smith that first semester back in spring 1954 was reduced in a number of ways. First, she was given a private room at Lawrence House. Second, her house duties were limited to one—she was to deliver the housemother her breakfast tray every morning. Third, she enrolled in only three classes—Nineteenth- Century Intellectual History, Tolstoy and Dostoevsky, and American Fiction 1830–1900. When she returned, her classmates had naturally heard about her as the nationally published writer and *Mademoiselle* guest editor who had tried to kill herself over the summer. Sylvia claimed in letters to friends that she was not disappointed to not be graduating with her class that spring. Instead, she found one or two close friends with whom she could talk openly about her experience and concentrated on getting back into the swing of school. That said, it is perhaps telling that she marked the following passage from *War and Peace*:

> To be enthusiastic had become her pose in society, and at times even when she had, indeed, no inclination to be so, she was enthusiastic so as not to disappoint the expectations of those who knew her.[11]

On the left margin, Plath writes, "Ah, yes!"

Reading aside, Sylvia did not stay in her room and brood when she came back to Smith. She went out to readings and on dates. She read novels such as *Sister Carrie* and *Crime and Punishment* for her classes, and even went back to New York to visit friends and have lunch with Cyrilly Abels in the Ivy Room at the Drake Hotel. While in New York, she went to the Metropolitan Museum, seeing a show of American painters Sargent, Whistler, and Cassatt. She also visited the Museum of Modern Art and saw the William Inge play, *Picnic*, starring Paul Newman and Sandra Church. That spring she also dyed her hair platinum blond à la Marilyn Monroe, an act she told her mother she performed as a sign of her new, more adventurous personality. The new hair color may also have been an act denoting a new glamour-seeking shift in attitude, marking a line in time between the days when she guarded her reputation because society dictated that she do so and this new era of her life when she believed she was more in control of her own choices and sensuality.

By April, she was writing poems again, something she had not attempted since before the experience at *Mademoiselle* almost a year before. She revised an old sonnet, "The Dead," and wrote another called "Doom of Exiles." *The Smith Review*, which she would have been editing had she not had her breakdown, published four of her poems in its spring issue—

"Admonitions," "Never to Know More Than You Should," "Verbal Calisthenics," and "Denouement." *Harper's* published "Doomsday" in May.

By the end of the spring semester, 1954, Sylvia did not graduate with
her class, but she had received a $1,200 scholarship to attend Smith the
following year. It was the largest scholarship Smith offered. In addition,
she received a scholarship to attend Harvard Summer School, the same
summer school she had not attended after New York the previous summer.
She had chosen her senior thesis topic—Dostoevsky, not Joyce as she had
once considered, and she again garnered excellent grades—American Fiction, A; Russian Literature, A; European History, A-. She was elected
president of Alpha Phi Kappa and won a $20 poetry prize for "Doom of
Exiles."

With money no longer an immediate concern for the fall or for summer
school, Sylvia could relax for the first few weeks that summer until summer school began on July 1. She vacationed at Eastham on the Cape with
her family and was a bridesmaid in a friend's wedding. While at the Cape,
she saw Dick Norton in Orleans and further convinced herself that she
could never marry him. By now, she thought she was in love with Gordon
Lameyer, a Naval Officer from Wellesley, though she continued to date
many other men, recording all of her exploits in continuing detail in her
copious journals.

When she moved to Cambridge for Harvard's Summer School, she
rented an apartment with three women she knew from Lawrence House.
She enrolled in two courses—German and Nineteenth-Century Novel,
the latter course being taught, ironically, by the same Frank O'Connor
who had rejected her for the writing class the summer before. For this class
she had a heavy reading load of novels such as Austen's *Emma* and *Pride
and Prejudice*, Stendhal's *The Charterhouse Parma*, Balzac's *Eugénie
Grandet*, Dickens's *Bleak House*, Trollope's *The Last Chronicle of Barset* and
Phineas Finn, Flaubert's *Madame Bovary*, Tolstoy's *The Cossacks*, Tur-
genev's *On the Eve*, and Twain's *Huckleberry Finn*.

One day outside on the steps of Widener Library, she and Nancy
Hunter from Lawrence House at Smith met a professor who was in Cambridge for the summer doing research. He asked the women if they would
like to go for coffee. Having made a pact that they would not turn down
dates or offers for free food on their limited budgets for the summer, the
women went with him to the coffee shop. He introduced himself as
Edwin, a biology professor from another East Coast college, and proceeded to talk almost nonstop about his work. Both Sylvia and Nancy
began to wonder which of them he was more interested in when he asked
for their telephone number.

When he called, he asked for Nancy, and the two made a date. Instead of going out to dinner, as she expected, Nancy was taken to Edwin's apartment. When she told him she was uncomfortable with this arrangement, he told her she would be perfectly safe; his landlady was at home next door, and he would leave the door open if it would help her feel more at ease. Sometime during the evening when Nancy was not looking, he closed the door. The evening ended with Nancy being chased around the couch in a manner not unlike a Keystone Cops comedy. Nancy demanded to be taken home and did not want to see him again. After telling Sylvia of her experience, Nancy was surprised to hear her talking with him longer and longer on the phone when he called looking for Nancy. Soon, Sylvia was dating him, and he began taking her to her regular meetings with her psychiatrist. In a memoir she wrote years later, *A Closer Look at Ariel: A Memory of Sylvia Plath*, Nancy relates a frightening incident that occurred with Sylvia and Edwin one night.

One morning Nancy awoke to find that Sylvia's bed had not been slept in. Though this concerned her, she surmised Sylvia must have spent the night at Edwin's. She was surprised when the telephone rang and it was Edwin. He informed her that Sylvia had been sick at his apartment the night before, and that the doctor advised her to stay where she was for the night but that she would be home soon. When Nancy asked what was wrong with her, Edwin admitted that she had suffered a hemorrhage. Nancy was not sure what to think, especially given her bad experience with Edwin. There was something about the look in his eye and the way he had chased her around his apartment that had struck her as being more sinister than mere horseplay. She believed he was dangerous.

When Sylvia returned to the girls' apartment, she looked terrible. As she sat at the dinner table, it became clear that something was dreadfully wrong. She went to the bathroom, and when Nancy checked on her, she found Sylvia lying in a pool of blood. When she told her they should call a doctor, Sylvia became hysterical. She did not want a doctor. When Nancy asked her which doctor she had seen the night before, Sylvia told her that she had used a false name out of fear that her name would end up in the papers again as it had the previous year over her breakdown. Nancy asked her to tell her the name of the doctor and the false identity, and she could refer to her by that name when she called. Sylvia sobbed and told her that she did not remember the name she used, and that Edwin had raped her, and the act had torn her inside.

Nancy called the doctor Sylvia had seen, and he gave her some home remedies to try to stop the bleeding, but they did not stop it for long. Finally, Nancy called Edwin and demanded that he take them to the hospital. There, a doctor managed to get Sylvia's bleeding under control. Nancy was furious with Edwin. When they got out of the car at their apartment and he said he would call the next day to see how Sylvia was, Nancy spat back at him not to bother.

To Nancy's dismay, Sylvia went back to seeing Edwin within a week. Though the relationship did not last past the summer of 1954, some observers believe it set in motion a pattern of Sylvia tolerating men who treated her badly, including those who would later hit her, spank her, or be otherwise violent toward her. Perhaps her attempt at gaining the sexual freedom she believed men enjoyed had backfired to the point that through her experimentation she gave certain men a different, dangerous kind of power over her altogether.

Oddly, when Sylvia told Gordon Lameyer about the affair with Edwin in early August, soft-pedaling the abuse to rough fondling rather than rape, Gordon agreed to let it go, even though by then he thought of himself and Sylvia as unofficially engaged. By the end of that month, they were close to marriage. In the few weeks after summer school and before she returned to Smith for her senior year, Sylvia thought about the pulls of marriage, family, and career. It is interesting to note that if she had been raped, the incident did not bring on another episode of her illness to the severity that it had been triggered by the rejection of her place in the creative writing class the previous summer.

Back at Lawrence House, Sylvia again roomed with Nancy Hunter. Her classes that fall were Shakespeare, Intermediate German, and her senior thesis. She also began drafting an application for a Fulbright Scholarship toward her goal of graduate study at Oxford or Cambridge. Her senior thesis would be a study of the use of the double in Dostoevsky's *The Double* and *The Brothers Karamazov*. Within weeks of working on these projects, she was back in the infirmary with a respiratory infection, a cycle that had already been repeated several times by now. Gordon Lameyer came to visit her.

When she was released again, Sylvia was asked by *The Smith Alumnae Quarterly* to write an article on Alfred Kazin, that semester's Neilson Professor in the English Department. During their interview, Kazin became impressed with Sylvia's publication history and invited her to sit in on his creative writing class. When she attended and impressed him above the 10 other students who were enrolled with her responses to discussion of the short stories they were considering, Kazin convinced Plath to join the class. As the author of *On Native Ground* and *A Walker in the City*, his reputation was too important for Sylvia to pass up the opportunity to study with him, so she added his class to her workload.

As she worked on her thesis, she continued to write odd articles for spare money. From what she learned in Kazin's class, Sylvia wrote her first short story that fall in nearly two years. She wrote to Gordon that she would always be grateful for the accident of interviewing Kazin that landed her in his class, where she was learning so much about writing. Soon, however, her workload built up again to the point where she wrote him that the only time she would have to see him for the next few months would be at Thanksgiving dinner. Gordon's patience with her was wearing thin.

To prepare for her Fulbright interviews, Sylvia changed her hair color to walnut brown, which she apparently thought gave her a more serious appearance. Professor Joyce Homer interviewed her for Oxford; Professor Mary Ellen Chase for Cambridge. *Harper's* published her poem, "Go Get the Goodly Squab" in November, eliciting an article about her in the Wellesley *Townsman* for having three poems published by the magazine within one year. In the middle of that month, Cyrilly Abels wrote to let her know that her poem "Parallax" had earned an honorable mention in *Mademoiselle's* Dylan Thomas Poetry Contest. In addition to the workload that kept her from seeing Gordon on the weekends that fall when he wanted to get together, Sylvia had a new love interest—a young man from Britain named Richard Sassoon.

Despite her many and varied male interests, however, Sylvia kept working hard. The year is striking because it is one of the few for which she did not use up writing energy by keeping a journal, though at least a partial calendar for the period survives. She finished the rough draft of her thesis by December and entered *Vogue's* Prix de Paris competition. She was back on the editorial board of *The Smith Review,* which published her poem, "Circus in Three Rings," and a short story, "In the Mountains." For the Fulbright and additional backup scholarships of the Radcliffe and Woodrow Wilson awards, she was getting names together and asking her professors for letters of recommendation. Mary Ellen Chase, Elizabeth Drew, Newton Arvin, Professors Kazin and George Gibian all wrote on her behalf. In addition, Dr. Barnhouse dealt with the question of her mental stability for study abroad by writing her a recommendation to send along with her applications as well.

In the spring semester of her senior year, 1955, Sylvia went back to Smith early in January and entered the infirmary with a sinus infection that kept her there for a week. During this stay, she wrote five poems and held court with visitors. One of these was a man sent by Alfred Kazin, an editor named Peter Davison from Harcourt, Brace who asked her to keep his publishing house in mind should she ever complete a novel. Before classes began, Sylvia dropped off her thesis to be typed; it was titled *The Magic Mirror: A Study of the Double in Two of Dostoevsky's Novels*. Her advisor, Professor Gibian, called it a masterpiece. She also sent out the new poems she had written to *The New Yorker*. Her classes during her last semester at Smith were: Shakespeare, Intermediate German, Twentieth-Century American Novel, a one-hour independent study in Theory and Practice of Poetics, and Honors hours. *Vogue* sent her notice that she reached the finals in the Prix de Paris, which meant that she next had to write a 10-page composition on Americana. If anyone thought Sylvia might allow herself an easy last semester of "senioritis," enjoying her youth and last weeks of college by not working quite as hard, they were badly mistaken. She did, however, decide to drop German, which she did not need to graduate, to allow her more time to focus on her writing. Ironically, German was the subject her father had taught many years earlier at Boston College and that her mother once taught in high school.

Given her credentials, Sylvia was shocked when her interview at Harvard did not go well for the Woodrow Wilson Fellowship. She thought the committee seemed biased in favor of male applicants and told her mother of her fears afterwards. Sure enough, she received a letter rejecting her application. In the meantime, she received acceptances into both Oxford and Cambridge Universities, which left her overjoyed. Her relationship with Sassoon had made her more curious than ever about Britain and life in England. Sylvia had begun making clandestine trips to New York City with him to enjoy French restaurants, Japanese films, and Russian plays. Strangely, Sassoon's letters to her suggest that their relationship was another of Sylvia's where she was mistreated by a man in a violent way. The letters contain innuendo about his spanking her and hitting her, perhaps as part of an unhealthy, sadist-masochistic form of lovemaking. At the same time that she was about to graduate with honors from Smith, she was living a secret life of this kind behind closed doors. Perhaps the doubling theme of her senior thesis had taken on a personal significance to her. As much as she appeared to stay interested in Sassoon, however, she continued to date several other men and keep her ties to Gordon Lameyer.

In March 1955, Sylvia wrote a piece for *Mademoiselle* about Smith's symposium on the Mid-Century Novel, which featured speakers such as Alfred Kazin and Saul Bellow. She became ill enough later in the month that she checked into the infirmary again for two days. After spring break, she participated in the Irene Glascock Poetry Contest at Mount Holyoke in South Hadley. The contest required that student poets stay at a dormitory on campus, hear advice about writing from the three judges, and read their own poetry in front of the judges and an audience at an evening gathering. The judges that year were John Ciardi, Wallace Fowlie, and Marianne Moore. *The Christian Science Monitor* interviewed the contestants and photographed each of them with Ms. Moore. At the reading, when it was her turn, Plath read "Winter Words," "Epitaph," "Lament," "Verbal Calisthenics," "April Aubade," "Love Is a Parallax," "*Danse macabre*," and "Two Lovers and a Beachcomber by the Real Sea." The day after the reading, the contestants were given breakfast in bed, and they recorded their poems for the campus radio station. After attending a forum on translation and a luncheon in their honor, the contestants were allowed to leave. Sylvia ended up tying with William Key Whitman for first prize of the competition; the two split the $100 winnings.

On Monday back at Smith, Sylvia was delighted to see that *The Christian Science Monitor* had put her picture with Marianne Moore in its pages and published her poem, "April Aubade." She took Ms. Moore's comments on her poetry for the mixed review that it was. She was informed that Moore "...commends your spirit, patience, craftsmanship, and strong individuality" and her main criticism "is of a too adjectival manner at times bordering on formula."[12] Mixed reviews were part of the game as a writer, Sylvia knew. She had just received a similar response from *The Atlantic Monthly* about her *Circus in Three Rings* poetry manuscript that she put together from her poetry writing independent study. Editor Edward Weeks tried to persuade her to rewrite the first and last stanzas of one of the poems so that it would live up to the beauty of the second. He urged her with a payment of $25 and an enticement that the magazine might publish a revision.

Sylvia did not know what to make of *The Atlantic Monthly* offer at first. She wrote to her mother that she thought Weeks's comments were paternalistic, and she did not want to change her work as much as he described. Still, she was offered a chance to have her work appear in one of the most respected literary magazines in the nation, so she decided to rework the poems in her own way and resubmit, letting Weeks know that she had just tied in the Glascock competition. In the meantime, she won the Alpha Phi Kappa Award, the Alpha Award in Creative Writing, and the $100 Christopher Prize. On May 4, she appeared at a literary festival in Kingston, New York, where she read her work to an audience of 700 students from across the state and judged a creative writing contest.

The crowning glory of the golden schoolgirl's academic career surely came when she graduated from Smith in the spring of 1955. Plath won one of only 12 honorable mentions in *Vogue*'s Prix de Paris, and she received a letter of invitation for a job at Condé Nast. At the last assembly at the college, she earned the following awards: the Elizabeth Babcock Poetry Prize, the Ethel Olin Corbin Prize for "Second Winter," the Marjorie Hope Nicholson Prize for best senior thesis, which she shared with another student, and the Academy of American Poets Prize. She also won the Clara French Prize for the most outstanding English student of the graduating class, was a member of Phi Beta Kappa, and would graduate as one of only four summa cum laude graduates in her class.

Near this same time, she learned that *Mademoiselle* bought "Two Lovers and a Beachcomber by the Real Sea," which it planned to publish in August, and *The Atlantic Monthly* had accepted "Circus in Three Rings," which it planned to publish the same month. The spring issue of *The Smith Review* contained her poem *"Danse macabre"* and her short story "Superman and Paula Brown's New Snowsuit." To top it all off, she received a letter from the State Department that she had been accepted as a Fulbright Scholar to study literature at Cambridge University in England. The Fulbright covered almost all her expenses for travel, tuition, and living costs. Sylvia described the next few days as feeling as though she were walking on air.

Graduation day was June 6, 1955, a pleasant early summer day. One of the honorary degree recipients that year was poet Marianne Moore, and she sat on the stage with the others. Former Illinois governor Adlai Stevenson gave the commencement address. Despite the rigors of their educations, Stevenson's advice to the all-female graduates was about working hard at establishing a creative marriage.

Aurelia Plath sat in the audience as her daughter received her diploma. She almost did not make it. For several weeks, she had been laid up in the hospital from complications associated with her ulcer. She had traveled several miles lying on a mattress in the back of a friend's station wagon in order to attend her daughter's college graduation. That her daughter's many academic and publishing successes nearly cost both of them their lives probably did not occur to her that day. Instead, she watched with pride as her golden schoolgirl daughter lined up alphabetically with the other Ps and accepted her diploma with a major in English. The English degree and career as a writer that Aurelia had been denied so many years before by her father and her husband was finally won back for her by her daughter. Only time would tell if the price paid had been too high for both of them.

NOTES

1. Sylvia Plath, *The Unabridged Journals of Sylvia Plath, 1950–1962*, ed. Karen V. Kukil. (New York: Random House, 2000) p. 8.

2. E-mail interview with 1955 Smith alumnus and Plath contemporary, Polly (Ormsby) Longsworth.

3. Qtd. in Paul Alexander, *Rough Magic: A Biography of Sylvia Plath* (New York: Viking Press, 1991) p. 81.

4. Qtd. in Alexander, *Rough Magic*, p. 87.

5. Qtd. in Alexander, *Rough Magic*, p. 87.

6. Plath, *Unabridged Journals*, p. 141.

7. Plath, *Unabridged Journals*, p. 141.

8. Plath, *Mademoiselle*, August 1953, p. 235.

9. Qtd. in Linda Wagner-Martin, *Sylvia Plath: A Biography* (New York: St. Martin's Press, 1987), p. 104.

10. Qtd. in Wagner-Martin, *Sylvia Plath: A Biography*, p. 99.

11. Leo Tolstoy, *War and Peace* (New York: Modern Library, n.d.), p. 2.

12. Qtd. in Alexander, *Rough Magic*, p. 155.

Haven House party for first-year students, May 1951 (Mortimer Rare Book Room, Smith College)

Sylvia Plath and Joan Cantor at Nauset Beach, Cape Cod, Massachusetts, August 1952 (Mortimer Rare Book Room, Smith College)

Marianne Moore talking to Sylvia Plath, April 15, 1955 (Mortimer Rare Book Room, Smith College, Gordon Converse/1995 © The Christian Science Monitor)

Studio portrait of Sylvia Plath by Eric Stahlberg, 1955 (Mortimer Rare Book Room, Smith College Archives, © Smith College)

Sylvia Plath with her typewriter in Yorkshire, England, 1956 (Mortimer Rare Book Room, Smith College)

Chapter 5

A POET'S LIFE AND A POET'S WIFE (1956–1961)

Graduation from Smith College in June of 1955 did not end Sylvia's fascination with formal education. That fall she headed to Cambridge on a Fulbright Scholarship to study English Literature. She hoped to write, travel, and have different adventures and experiences. Several men in her life still vied for her commitment, but Sylvia was not ready to settle down to marriage. There was too much world out there yet to see and experience. Despite her infatuation and relationships with different men, she had not yet met the one she felt earned her faithfulness and devotion. That would all change in England, too.

The summer before her trip abroad, Sylvia visited her mother in the hospital, and when she was released, Sylvia took her to the Cape to celebrate Grammy and Grampy Schober's 50th wedding anniversary. She served as Ruth Freeman's maid of honor in her wedding to Arthur Geissler at Saint John's Episcopal Church in Winthrop. She also took stock of her poetry writing—she counted over 220 poems that she had written by now, many of which had already appeared in national publications. She did a little traveling—Washington, D.C., where she saw the Washington Monument, the National Gallery, the White House, Supreme Court, Capitol, and the Library of Congress. She also spent some more time in New York where she went to Bloomingdale's and Rockefeller Center. She saw Gordon Lameyer, when it appeared more evident than ever that their relationship would probably not survive her first trip overseas. She also dated Peter Davison, the young editor from Harcourt, Brace who had visited her in the Smith infirmary.

Before going overseas, Sylvia made her rounds of good-byes, seeing
Olive Higgins Prouty and Mary Ellen Chase and spending some down-
time with Warren at Crane's Beach in early September. On the 12th,
Warren drove her to New York. On the 14th, she kissed Warren and
boarded the *Queen Elizabeth II*, which pulled out of New York Harbor at 9
o'clock that evening. As the boat left the harbor, she wrote "farewell to
Manhattan" in her tiny calendar and watched as America receded over
the horizon and an endless sea opened up before her.

CAMBRIDGE

It took three days for the *Queen Elizabeth II* to make the trip across the
ocean. On the ship, Sylvia met Carl Shakin, and the two spent time together ballroom dancing on the ship and sitting on the deck. When the
boat pulled into port first at Cherbourgh, France, the two went ashore for
an enjoyable afternoon. The ship made its way to Southampton, England,
where Sylvia and the Fulbright students boarded trains that took them to
Waterloo Station in London.

Carl remained Sylvia's companion for her first few days in London.
They went to see several plays, including *Waiting for Godot*. On September 24, she moved in with four other Fulbright women to a fourth floor
room at the YWCA for the few days until the beginning of her Cambridge
term on October 1. At that time, she boarded a train and headed north to
her college, Newnham, to get settled in and begin classes.

Sylvia imported a bicycle to get herself around the town of Cambridge.
She loved the sights and sounds of the place, the different colleges that
made up the university with their stately, old exteriors, the River Cam,
the rose gardens, bookshops, fish-and-chips diners, and narrow cobblestone streets. Her living quarters were in Whitstead, a large house near
Newnham where 10 female students shared the space. Hers was a single
room in the attic that had a window seat where she could read and look
down on the Whitstead gardens. It all seemed very pleasant to the excited
student.

Knowing that she needed to meet people in her new surroundings,
Sylvia joined some activities right away, including the Amateur Dramatic
Club, where she tried out for roles such as Rosalind in Shakespeare's *As
You Like It* and Camille in Tennessee Williams's *Camino Real*. Men out-
numbered women ten to one in Cambridge, so Sylvia did not need to look
far for a date when she wanted one. With the other Fulbright students also
open to meeting one another and helping one another become acclimated, it seemed as though it would not take long to form friendships.

As one who adored the sea and sun, however, it also did not take long for Sylvia to dislike the Cambridge weather. She had a sinus infection as early as October 12 and checked into the campus hospital for relief. At Smith, the normal treatment she took to fight back the chronic infection included penicillin and, surprisingly, cocaine spray, but at Cambridge, she was given nothing stronger than aspirin. The severe pain in her head continued. In the campus hospital, Sylvia also found the meals tasteless and the nurses rude compared to what she had been used to at Smith. She left the hospital and went to a National Health Services physician, Dr. Bevan, who gave her a prescription.

That fall, Sylvia saw the royal couple up close. It was a rare occurrence to see royalty, especially so for an American. Queen Elizabeth and the Duke of Edinburgh came to Newnham to celebrate the opening of a new veterinary laboratory. Sylvia stood along the greeting line of Newnham women as the couple walked between them. They had glasses of sherry and made a presentation. Sylvia was enthralled with them both, so much so that when they went to leave, she followed them out in the pouring rain to watch them get into a car that took them to Trinity College for lunch.

Newnham academic years operated on trimesters rather than semesters, but that still meant a break at Christmastime. Sylvia used the break to visit France, meeting Sassoon in Paris. She loved Paris even more than she did London. They visited the Champs-Elysées, the Seine Chapel in the Ile de la Cité, the Rue de la Paix, and the Louvre, where Plath marveled at Brueghel, *Winged Victory*, and the *Mona Lisa*. She and Sassoon enjoyed watching the children at the Garden of the Tuileries, took in an Impressionist exhibit at the Orangerie, walked along the Seine, and saw two French films and two plays. On Christmas Day, Sassoon took her to Notre Dame Cathedral. Sitting quietly in a pew underneath the spectacular rose window her first Christmas away from home, Sylvia thought about her mother, Warren, and all of those back home she loved.

For New Year's, the couple went to Nice along the Mediterranean. From their room, they could see the snow-capped peaks of the Alps, the blue Mediterranean, and orange and olive groves. The rented a motorbike and wound their way to Ventimiglia, Italy, and Monte Carlo. Another day they motorbiked to Vence, where Sylvia wanted to see a Matisse chapel. She got out her sketchpad and began to draw it. The gate to the chapel said that it was closed, and as she drew it, Sylvia began to cry, thinking of the beauty of the sunlight and how it must look inside with the stained glass windows casting different colors along the pews and how she would never be able to see it. Seemingly out of nowhere while she was thinking this, the mother superior appeared and opened the gate to allow her in. In a rare moment of spiritual grace, since she was not a believer, Sylvia walked into the center of the blue, green, and yellow filtered light, the colors of sea, sun, and sky inside the chapel and lowered herself to her knees.

Even before their romantic trip to Paris and the Mediterranean, Sylvia was beginning to think that she did not want to date any other men besides Sassoon. Consequently, she was shocked and hurt when they returned to Paris and Sassoon admitted to her that he planned on seeing other women after she returned to Cambridge. In truth, he was nearly engaged to a Swiss woman. Devastated, Sylvia flew back to England where she barely enjoyed the Christmas gift Gordon had sent to her, an autographed copy of poet Richard Wilbur's *Misanthrope*.

TED HUGHES

When the second term started in mid-January, Sylvia decided to set aside her romantic and social concerns and concentrate on her studies and her writing. She wrote a short story about her Vence experience called "The Matisse Chapel" and submitted it to *The New Yorker*. She worked on her renewal application for the Fulbright (only 10 percent of renewal applications were approved), and she became determined to write at least two hours every day. Even so, she wrote to her mother that she was very unhappy. *The New Yorker* turned down her story in two weeks with a form rejection letter. Grammy Schober had recently been diagnosed with stomach cancer. Sylvia wrote her grandmother a heartfelt letter and continued seeing a psychiatrist. One of her complaints she discussed in her therapy sessions was that she knew no elders in England to turn to for advice and counsel as she had at Smith and Wellesley. No one looked out for her. Things did not get any better when her first poems printed in England, in a local college publication, *Chequer*, in January 1956, did not receive good reviews. One of these poems was "'Three Caryatids without a Portico' by Hugo Robus: A Study in Cultural Dimensions."

In fact, one reviewer in another small student literary publication, the *Broadsheet*, labeled her a fraud, a secret fear she had always carried around with her, even through all of her previous successes. The rebuke hit a nerve. "Quaint and eclectic artfulness," the student reviewer said. "My better half tells me 'Fraud, fraud,' but I will not say so; who am I to know how beautiful she may be?"[1] Putting evaluation of her work beside evaluation of her attractiveness as a female, however, was all the challenge

Sylvia needed to rise up and deal with the criticism head-on. She had rarely had trouble attracting men, and this was a student publication, after all; her work had been published commercially in the States. She soon learned, however, that the artistic, commercial, and academic literary worlds in the smaller country of England were tightly woven together. Commercial publishers regularly scouted for new talent among academic publications.

That February, some students and other poets around Cambridge were establishing yet another small literary publication, something they called *St. Botolph's Review*. Their inaugural issue came out that month and featured poems by Daniel Huws, the reviewer who had dismissed Plath's poems in *Chequer*, Ted Hughes, David Ross, and others. Sylvia picked up one of the small print run of 75 copies and took it back to her room. She was immediately taken by the quality of some of the stories and poems. When she was invited to attend the launch party that evening, she set about her goal of meeting Daniel Huws face-to-face and confronting him about his bad review of her work. Before going to the party, she prepared for battle by memorizing several of the poems in *St. Botolph's* and dressing seductively in red party shoes with a red hairband and earrings. If he wanted to see if she was beautiful, she was going to give him the chance to see so for himself.

The party on Saturday night, February 25, 1956, was in full swing by the time she got to Falcon Yard with her date and climbed upstairs to the Women's Union. A jazz combo wailed loud music over the heads of Cambridge students and local poets, writers, and antiestablishment intellectuals. Sylvia worked the room, fueling her courage with whiskey until she found Daniel Huws. When she found him, a short, pale, and freckled student, she felt he was not so imposing a threat after all and decided he was not worth the effort. Instead, as she cut in and danced with men she found attractive, she set her sights on a tall, lanky, good-looking man across the room and learned that his name was Ted Hughes.

Unlike other properly dressed Cambridge men of the 1950s, Hughes stood out for his bohemian style; he wore old, raggedy black corduroys and greasy hair. He also had a deep voice that attracted women and was known around Cambridge for his successes with them. Hughes caught her eye, and though they had both come to the party with someone else, he made his way over to Sylvia and looked hard into her eyes. Shouting over the loud music, Sylvia recited his "Law in the Country of the Cats," a poem she had memorized from *St. Botolph's*. The poem features two men who hate each other on their first meeting and alludes to themes of D. H. Lawrence and Sigmund Freud, writers and thinkers both Ted and Sylvia had read. Soon, over the blaring jazz music, Ted caught on to what she was doing and shouted back, "You like?"[2] This quick conversation immediately told them that they had read and responded to the same things and picked up on the same vibes; there was an immediate connection.

Before long, Ted backed her into an adjoining room, poured her some brandy, and apologized for his comrade's bad review of her poems in the *Broadsheet*. He did not tell her he shared the reviewer's opinion. They bantered back and forth, Sylvia excited and feisty, challenging him, the chemistry between them palpable. Suddenly, according to Plath's detailed journal account, Ted kissed Sylvia hard on the mouth then ripped off her hairband and earrings. When he kissed her neck, she retaliated by biting him long and hard on the cheek, drawing blood. When they emerged back into the main room of the party, blood was running down his cheek. Though he was obligated to leave with his date and she with hers, he carried the scar of their first meeting for days afterwards.

Ted Hughes would say later that he thought that destiny had brought him and Sylvia Plath together. Born Edward James Hughes at 1 Aspinall Street, Mytholmroyd, West Yorkshire, on August 16, 1930, Hughes began writing poetry as an adolescent. He attributed the ominous, violent atmosphere in his poetry to stories his father told him about his service in World War I and to his experiences hunting small game with his brother on the moors. That was where he became familiar with the natural world that would provide him the subject matter and imagery for much of his work. Like Plath, he dreamed of becoming a great poet like his idols W. B. Yeats and D. H. Lawrence.

After serving in the Royal Air Force (RAF), Hughes graduated from Cambridge University a year and a half before Sylvia Plath arrived there. In early 1956, he had a job in London reading fiction submissions at the film company J. Arthur Rank. On the weekends, however, he still went to Cambridge to see his old poet friends who were mostly still students at the university. Unlike Plath, his work had appeared thus far only in small literary journals, but like her, he had not yet published a collection of his poetry. Recently, Hughes had applied for immigration to Australia where he hoped to hunt and fish with his older brother Gerald, who already lived there. As he considered what he would do for a living in that country, however, he kept asking for extensions on his application so that he could remain in England while he figured out his plans.

After their first meeting, Sylvia went home and wrote about it in her journal. She called him "that big, dark, hunky boy. ... The one man in the room who was as big as his poems."[3] She thought he was magnificent and dreamed of giving herself over to his power and artistry, but she knew he worked in London, and she did not expect to see him again. Two weeks later, however, Ted came back to Cambridge and asked one of his friends to help him find Sylvia's room. Throwing clumps of dirt at her window at 2 o'clock in the morning, Ted found out that Sylvia was out with another man and that he had also picked the wrong window. They did not meet again until the end of the second term in March, when Sylvia needed to vacate her room for the two-week holiday. She moved to London to stay in a hotel near Ted's apartment while she waited to go to Paris to see Richard Sassoon. Their next meeting was on March 23, 1956.

Neither Ted nor Sylvia wanted to make the first move to see each other, so Ted arranged for go-betweens to bring Sylvia out to a pub that poets frequented, the Lamb on Conduit Street; the friends then suggested that they go visit Ted in his apartment. When Sylvia arrived, the friends left the two alone. When they returned, they found Hughes and Plath sitting in two separate chairs drawn face-to-face to one another, Ted leaning toward Sylvia, with both whispering in the short distance to one another. Sylvia seemed agitated about something. Later, Ted's *Birthday Letters* suggested that she had told him about her suicide attempt in 1953 that night. Soon Ted offered to walk her back to her hotel, where they spent a passionate night.

Despite the magnetism Sylvia felt for Ted, she still made her way afterwards to Paris and looked for Richard Sassoon. While there, she also gathered notes about the city for a novel she hoped to write about her Fulbright years. She sent Hughes a postcard before she went to Rome on April 6 with a picture of Rousseau's *Snake Charmer*. Hughes was prepared to be more aggressive in the relationship—he sent her two letters which surprisingly reached her during her travels on the Continent, the second one containing a 12-line poem. When she returned from this trip, she went straight to Ted, and they were a couple from that moment on.

It did not take long for them to begin discussing marriage. In *Her Husband: Hughes and Plath—A Marriage*, Diane Middlebrook states that it was Sylvia who proposed. Because Sylvia was afraid that the Fulbright frowned on students marrying while on scholarship, she wanted to wait until she finished to marry. Ted was still deciding what to do with his career—at one time he thought of going to Spain, still on the way to Australia, and Sylvia was going to go with him. As they discussed their futures, Sylvia talked Ted out of going to Australia, and he let his application lapse. She suggested he teach in Spain while she finished at Cambridge. While their plans were still up in the air, Aurelia Plath paid a visit to her daughter.

Warren was still a Harvard student, but he happened to be in Europe that spring as well. He was working on a project in Austria. With Sylvia in England, it seemed to Aurelia a good time to make her first vacation abroad after so many years of work. She had heard about Ted in letters from Sylvia, so no doubt she wanted to meet this man her daughter seemed to put on a different level than all of the other men she had dated. Olive Higgins Prouty had written to Sylvia that she was unsure Ted was good for her. From Sylvia's letters, Prouty thought he sounded too much like Dylan Thomas, with a violent past and history that she discouraged Sylvia from thinking she could change. Despite this warning by her benefactor, hearing that her mother was on her way, Sylvia wrote that she looked forward to showing her around London and Cambridge and to introducing her to Ted Hughes.

For some unknown reason, soon after Aurelia arrived that summer, the couple made a hasty decision to get married, and Aurelia agreed. Perhaps Aurelia sensed that, married or not, the couple was already headed toward living together. From what she had seen of Ted, he was charming, and she could see why her daughter had fallen for him. The couple gathered the necessary paperwork and said their vows at the Church of St. George the Martyr in London on June 16, 1956, with Aurelia the only family member in attendance. Sylvia wore a pink suit that her mother bought her and carried a pink rose that was a gift from Ted. It so happened that their wedding day was Bloomsday, June 16, the day on which James Joyce's novel *Ulysses* takes place.

Ted's friends were surprised that he married the American Sylvia Plath. They thought her too flashy for his taste, too loud and too aggressive. They did not like her, and they did not even like her poetry. They thought that a more likely partner for Ted Hughes, as a poet who wrote about earthy subjects like hunting and animals, would be a woman from the countryside, one who appreciated nature as he did and understood its possibilities for exploration of deep, spiritual dimensions. Plath was too slick, they said, too commercial. In fact, for the May 26, 1956, issue of Cambridge's *Varsity* magazine, she had posed as a model for several photographs. In two, she is wearing flouncy cocktail dresses, in another two a polka-dotted bathing suit and high heels. This image did not strike Hughes's bohemian friends as one befitting a serious poet.

One of the aspects about Ted that interested Sylvia besides her physical attraction to him and their common interest and experience in poetry was that she sensed she could learn a lot from him. She admired his work and saw a certain groundedness in it that her own lacked. They also had complementary skills in getting on in the world. Ted taught Sylvia how to prepare food on a hearth from freshly caught fish and raw vegetables he brought home. She typed and packaged his writing for submission to publishers. They both liked to sketch, and one of their favorite games was completing quotations. One would start a quote from literature, and the other would finish it. In ways such as these and others that began later, the two poets forged a relationship that enhanced the poems of them both. Years later, in the early twenty-first century, analysts would begin looking through their letters and poems for literary connections that illustrated the development of this symbiosis.

After their wedding, in another of several similarities that would exist between Sylvia's marriage to Ted and her mother's to Otto Plath, Aurelia accompanied the couple on their honeymoon trip to Paris. Ted made a quick trip home to Yorkshire first for provisions while Sylvia took her mother around London and Cambridge, but he did not notify his family of his marriage. When Sylvia learned of his secrecy, she was surprised and perplexed and asked him to write his family about it and tell them that they would visit them in Yorkshire once they returned later in the summer. One can only guess why the once confirmed bachelor was not yet ready to tell his family that he had hastily married an ambitious American poet. When his friends asked him the same question, he had only responded, why not?

Their plan for that first summer was to spend two weeks in Paris and six weeks in Spain. The time in Spain was to be a working vacation for them both. On limited funds, the strain of trying to work side by side in a strange environment might have pulled apart other new couples, but the Hugheses found it a mutual challenge they both enjoyed. They were beginning to settle on household responsibilities; both would cook, for example. For Ted's birthday on August 16, they each consulted a cookbook Sylvia had brought along, *The Joy of Cooking,* for how to prepare rabbit stew. Soon Sylvia was going through her cookbook trying new recipes in what Ted thought was a way to avoid writing. He wrote to his brother Gerald that his wife cooked for pleasure while he cooked only out of necessity.

When they settled into a routine, they split the day's household duties so that each of them had about six hours of work time. This plan seemed to suit both of them. Soon, as every married couple does, they began to find and try to adjust to one another's faults as living companions. Sylvia was difficult to live with in that she was possessive and sentimental. She planned everything, even the days when she would wash her hair were noted on her calendar, and when something did not seem to go as she planned, she needed reassurance that it was not a code red crisis. Ted was difficult to live with because he was grumpy, picked his nose, and gave no thought to his appearance, including washing his hair. He finally broke down and bought new clothes after Sylvia nagged him about it hard enough. More severe problems underlay these surface ones—Sylvia was susceptible to bouts of depression, jealousy, and anger; Ted could be cruel and apparently even violent.

Sylvia's view of their family planning involved she and Ted each publishing two books in four years, and then having two children. Like her mother before her, she encouraged her husband with his first book, a collection of poems, actually typing up the manuscript of *The Hawk in the Rain* for submission as her mother had edited Otto's book on bees. She took on much of the business side of their work, studying markets, collecting reviews, and preparing and sending out submissions.

In October 1956, Sylvia, still fearful that the Fulbright administrators would find out that she was married, returned to Cambridge and resumed her studies while Ted went to Yorkshire and stayed with his parents. He wrote her letters and began making recommendations about her poetry. In the meantime, she continued to have success in publishing. *Poetry* accepted all six poems she had submitted; *Granta* published her short story, "The Day Mr. Prescott Died;" and *The Christian Science Monitor* accepted "Sketchbook of a Spanish Summer."

Ted gave Sylvia a pack of tarot cards for her birthday. He had always had an interest in astrology and was now delving into tarot and Ouija boards. This became a theme throughout their marriage. When they began making a little more money as writers, Sylvia even purchased a crystal ball with which they would attempt to read their fortunes. Ted experimented with hypnosis as well. Once, when Sylvia was ill in Spain and could not sleep, he hypnotized her and gave her a suggestion that she would sleep and wake in the morning, completely well. Whether the suggestion or coincidence were at play, that is exactly what happened.

Finally, when she met some other Fulbright female students who were married, Sylvia got up the courage to notify her contacts about Ted. Rather than threaten to take away her scholarship, they simply offered her their congratulations. She and Ted established a home in a rented apartment at 55 Eltisley Avenue and tried different ways to make money. Ted taught for a brief time at a boys' school and consulted the Ouija board for bets on the weekly British football (soccer) pool. Sylvia continued to take in money in small amounts here and there for her writing; she also began to think about returning to America to show Ted around Wellesley and other places important to her and to teach for a while to store up some cash.

In the meantime, they received notice that Ted's *The Hawk in the Rain*, which Sylvia submitted to the first book competition at the Poetry Center of the 92nd Street Y in New York City, had won first place. This ensured that the book would be published. After some debate over inclusions and exclusions that judge Marianne Moore had suggested and Ted grappled with, the book was eventually accepted by Faber and Faber for publication in England. Sylvia was delighted that Ted's goal of a published book was reached first. Even back as far as in her high school scrapbook, she admitted being glad that a boy had won first prize in a spelling bee and she second because she always liked having a boy ahead of her. She assumed that her success would not be long behind. In April of 1957, her poems "Spinster" and "Black Rook in Rainy Weather" were accepted by *The London Magazine*, her first professional British acceptance.

NEWLYWEDS IN AMERICA

In late May 1957, Sylvia completed her exams at Cambridge and her Fulbright experience with the equivalent of a high B grade. That summer, she and Ted set out for America. Sylvia had accepted an instructor position at Smith, teaching three classes of freshman English each semester for one year. Aurelia threw a reception for her daughter and son-in-law in the backyard of 26 Elmwood Road. Family and friends came to wish Sylvia and her new husband well, even though by now the couple had already celebrated and passed their first wedding anniversary. As a gift, Aurelia had arranged for them to spend several weeks that summer at Eastham, Cape Cod, before Sylvia's teaching job would begin in Northampton.

While they were on the Cape, Ted's poetry started appearing in more journals and magazines. The winning of the first book prize had done much to propel his notoriety. His work now appeared in *The Spectator*, *The Nation*, *Poetry*, and *Harper's*. Not only that, but the prestigious magazine *The New Yorker*, to which Sylvia had been submitting work for years with not much better success than form letter rejections, accepted Ted's poem "The Thought-Fox." In just a few short months, partly from her help at marketing and submitting his work, Ted had surpassed most of the prizes and publishing accomplishments Sylvia had garnered over the last several years.

Try as she might, Sylvia fought writer's block on the Cape that summer. She tried writing one short story, "The Trouble-making Mother," and rewrote "The Laundromat Affair," but neither was published. She spent quite a bit of time writing a poem of nearly 600 lines that was a rhymed dialogue between personae named Sibyl and Leroy called "Dialogue over a Ouija Board," which she never even bothered to submit to any magazine.

She tried to mollify her disappointment by cooking, baking, and reading. That summer she read novels by Faulkner, Wolfe, and Henry James.

TEACHING AT SMITH

Sylvia's year teaching at Smith did not help her writing at all, either. As many English professors do, Sylvia found the task of grading dozens of freshman essays exhausting on top of teaching a full-time load of classes. The work left her drained and creatively empty. Her former professors, for the most part, who had so encouraged her as a student now passed by in the hall with a minimum hello; now that she was their colleague, she did not garner the attention she had as their student. She did have a publication or two that fall, but her writing had almost come to a halt.

Meanwhile, Ted's *The Hawk in the Rain* was published simultaneously by Faber and Faber in England and Harper and Brothers in the United States. The book received rave reviews in such important review journals as *Library Journal, The New Statesman, The New York Times*, the London *Times*, and the *Times Literary Supplement*. Still generally happy for her husband's success, the drain of teaching set alongside of it made Sylvia jealous of Ted for the first time in their relationship. Her old fear of losing her talent began to come back again as well. By the end of the fall semester, she became ill with pneumonia and had to cancel the last five days of her classes. Though Smith had renewed her contract for another year, Sylvia refused to sign on, and wondered how she would even manage to finish out the spring when she returned.

Ted also started teaching that spring, English and creative writing classes, at the University of Massachusetts at Amherst. Sylvia's possessiveness and jealousy crept from her husband's writing success to growing suspicions over his obvious love of attention from his female students. Rumors among the Smith faculty and students of Ted's blatantly enjoying the company of women down at Paradise Pond while waiting for his wife only accelerated when he became an instructor himself.

In February 1958, *Mademoiselle* accepted Sylvia's poem "November Graveyard," her first acceptance in nearly a year. *ARTNews* commissioned her to write poems about objects of art, and she set about this task with enthusiasm. By spring break, she felt ready to write again and wrote several poems based on works by artist Paul Klee. These poems included "Virgin in a Tree," "Perseus," "Battle-Scene," and "The Departure of the Ghost" (later renamed "The Ghost's Leavetaking"). During the same stretch of time, she wrote "The Disquieting Muses," "On the Decline of Oracles," "Snake-charmer," and "The Dream." Within eight days, she had written eight of her finest poems to date. By using art as her inspiration, she had found a new level to her voice.

By the end of the school year, Sylvia's suspicions of Ted had grown. On May 21, 1958, she finished teaching her last class at Smith. Despite her own feelings of inferiority at the front of the classroom, several students later said she was a good instructor, even brilliant. Still, she and Ted had agreed they would not return to teaching the following year but would move to Boston and write. That afternoon, despite not wanting to know the truth, she decided to act on her suspicions and the rumors she had overhead by walking across the campus and down by Paradise Pond to the road where the Smith women took their boyfriends. She knew the road well from her five years at Smith as a student herself. Sure enough, there she spotted her husband laughing and walking with a young student wearing Bermuda shorts. Seeing Sylvia, the student ran off, and the couple got into a huge argument that continued back at their apartment and escalated allegedly to the point of violence on both sides.

BOSTON

Somehow they made up, perhaps believing that leaving teaching would help. They enjoyed a few days in New York City, where Sylvia showed Ted the sights. Aurelia made dinner for them for their second wedding anniversary on June 16, 1958, and there she told them she was concerned about their both giving up their teaching positions. Aurelia was understandably worried. As a widow who had worked and scraped together a living her whole life by teaching and who saw that her two children were well educated, she naturally wanted to see them avoid having similar concerns about money. Together Ted and Sylvia were giving up an annual income for the following year of over $6,000, a sum that was not insignificant in those days and certainly was not so to Aurelia.

By the time they moved into their apartment at 9 Willow Street in Boston, Sylvia had reached a milestone in her publishing career that motivated her to tell her mother the couple had made the right decision not to return to teaching. For the first time in her life, *The New Yorker*, through editor Howard Moss, purchased two of her poems—"Mussel Hunter at Rock Harbor" and "Nocturne" for a total sum of $338. In those days, that amount of money paid for three months' rent on their Beacon Hill apartment. *The London Magazine* published her poems "Spinster" and "Black Rook in Rainy Weather." The *Sewanee Review* accepted "The Ghost's Leavetaking," and *The Christian Science Monitor* published her article, "Beach Plum Season on Cape Cod." It seemed that she was getting

back on track. Despite her successes, however, the couple's financial concerns soon reappeared that fall.

When she found herself in another writing dry spell in Boston, Sylvia
listed her name with a temporary employment agency. Ironically, the assignment she was sent out on as a part-time secretary was working at the
same psychiatric unit of Massachusetts General Hospital where she had
been taken following her suicide attempt five years earlier. In her job, she
typed patients' records and answered the telephone. About this same
time, she began seeing Dr. Barnhouse again for therapy. She had been trying to have a baby with no success. Writing was not going well, and
money was tight.

Though she worked at the hospital only two months, the case studies
she read while she typed along with reading more of Freud and undergoing her own private analysis with Dr. Barnhouse brought Sylvia to write a
short story called "Johnny Panic and the Bible of Dreams." Some say this
story is the best she ever wrote. Also, that fall, *The Ladies' Home Journal*
published her poem "Second Winter." It seemed that in her desire to be
the perfect writer, perfect wife, and perfect woman, Sylvia always had this
dual life in her work between writing what women's magazines published
and writing what was appreciated by the more traditional literary magazines. In therapy with Dr. Barnhouse, she came to understand one reason
why she may have reacted the way she did when she saw Ted talking with
the young woman at Smith by Paradise Pond. He was supposed to have
met Sylvia after her last class. She began to believe that he loved her but
that he was not there for her—which she realized was the way she viewed
her relationship with her father. Focusing on the theme of a dead father
also began to be an interest in her writing about this time.

In the spring semester, 1959, Plath began auditing Robert Lowell's creative writing seminar at Boston University. The experience was a good
one for her; she saw a way to shift her writing so that it concentrated not
on external subjects as much as internal, tougher ones. Poet Anne Sexton, who also had grown up in Wellesley, gone to Bradford High School,
and had mental problems, was in the workshop as well. Through her therapy with Dr. Barnhouse, Sylvia was seeing that her greatest fear was failure. She had to take on fear of failure in her marriage, in her art, and with
her mother to get more to the core of her writing self. It was a recognize-
ble step in the evolution of her voice and subject matter that would lead
toward the astounding poems she wrote for her collection, *Ariel,* a few
years later.

In the meantime, *Mademoiselle* ran a story called "Four Young Poets," of
which she and Ted were two. The story focused on how poets make ends

meet while doing their writing. Interviews with both Sylvia and Ted painted a rosier picture than the way things actually were. The magazine portrayed them as a couple that goes back to academia each time they run out of cash. That was partly true. Both had recently had stints teaching, and Sylvia explained for the magazine how taxing teaching had been on their writing. Lately, she had toyed with the idea of going to graduate school, getting a doctorate, and going into teaching full time, just because she thought that it was money problems that were making her and Ted so disagreeable with one another so frequently. She did not say this to the magazine.

On Sunday, March 8, 1959, Sylvia did something that Dr. Barnhouse had been encouraging her to do for some time as part of her therapy. She finally, for the first time, visited her father's grave. She and Ted rode a trolley to Winthrop, where Sylvia walked the streets reminiscing and getting up her courage to go to Winthrop Cemetery. When she did, she found the grave right away, since it was along the Azalea Path near the front gate in the newer section of the graveyard. She wrote in her journal that when she saw his gravestone that she wanted to dig her father up to prove to herself that he had actually existed. Her sadness was so great that she and Ted walked out of the cemetery, through Winthrop, and along the shore so far that they ended up at Deer Island where a prison guard told them they could go no farther.

In April, the Hugheses received good news. Ted had been awarded a Guggenheim Fellowship in the amount of $5,000. This money would see them through nearly the rest of the year in terms of living expenses. They had also been invited to Yaddo, a writers' colony in Saratoga Springs, New York, for the months of September, October, and November. The *Sewanee Review* accepted Sylvia's poem "Point Shirley," and *The New Yorker* took "Watercolor of Grantchester Meadows" and "Man in Black." Sylvia had just completed her first children's book, *The Bed Book*, and was negotiating with a publisher about revisions. Ted's first children's book, *Meet My Folks!* was accepted for publication at Faber and Faber by none other than T. S. Eliot. Despite these successes for herself and Ted, Sylvia was jealous of Anne Sexton's book deal with Houghton Mifflin, and she and Ted continued to argue.

That summer they borrowed a car supplied by Aurelia and drove across country for several weeks before they came back east and went to Yaddo. They wanted to reach Sylvia's Aunt Frieda (on her father's side) and Uncle Walter in Pasadena, California, camping at stops along the way. These stops included Sault Sainte Marie, Michigan; Yellowstone Park; and the Great Salt Lake. On the way back they took a southern route through Tennessee, where they met the editor and staff of the *Sewanee Review*. During one night camping, a bear broke into their car doing not an insignificant amount of damage. Sylvia wrote about the incident in a short story, "The Fifty-ninth Bear," which was later published in *The London Magazine* in February, 1961.

Sylvia did not know it when they began their trip, but she was finally pregnant after seeing a gynecologist for fertility issues and trying for some time. Perhaps it was the first meeting with her father's family in seeing Aunt Frieda that caused her to give the daughter who was born that name. Sylvia was taken with how closely Aunt Frieda looked like her father, the same shape of face and piercing blue eyes.

YADDO

The Hugheses took up their residencies at the writers' colony of Yaddo in early September 1959. Cabins and Victorian houses stood among the wooded grounds. Residents wrote during the day, took boxed lunches with them to their studies and worked, then attended readings or concerts and met with one another over shared evening meals if they chose. The staff took care of cooking and cleaning, leaving visiting writers time to do what they came there to do, which was write. Ted took up residence in a cabin to do his work, while Sylvia stayed at West House. The longer they stayed, the fewer residents remained at the colony, since most had to return to teaching jobs.

Sylvia acclimated to her surroundings first by reading with a writer's eye. She read and admired Eudora Welty, Katherine Anne Porter, Jean Stafford, Elizabeth Bishop, and Iris Murdoch. She read but did not like John Updike and Nadine Gordimer. She had several rejections during that fall, but also a few acceptances. *The New Yorker* purchased "A Winter's Tale," and *The London Magazine* took her short story "This Earth Our Hospital." A letter from James Michie at William Heinemann publishers in England asked to see her first volume of poems when she was ready. After several collections had been turned down by other publishers, Michie's interest gave Sylvia new hope.

She and Ted continued their practice of tapping into their imaginations through hypnosis or other concentration exercises. After one of these exercises, Sylvia wrote the poems "The Manor Garden" and "The Colossus." The latter poem was one of the most mature and sophisticated she had written yet. When she reordered and organized her collection once again, she chose for it the title *The Colossus and Other Poems*. Other poems she wrote at Yaddo include "Poem for a Birthday" and "The

Stones." The latter poem of these two caused Ted to say that she had turned a corner in her writing; "The Stones" was her best poem yet. Sylvia continued to work with Ted's suggestions. Another resident of Yaddo while they were there said that she deferred to him always, letting him speak first when they were with a group, letting him enter a room first. There was a quiet confidence about her during this period, the observer said, as though she knew she would get her turn.

RETURN TO ENGLAND

After Yaddo, the couple spent Thanksgiving with Aurelia in Wellesley then prepared to return to England. Sylvia was examined by a doctor, who confirmed that she was five months along in her pregnancy. Having spent two years in America, on December 12, 1959, the couple boarded the S. S. *United States* and headed back across the sea to England, promising Aurelia they would be back in another two years. Unfortunately, Sylvia would never return.

They settled in London. On February 5, as she anticipated the birth of her first baby, Sylvia was notified by James Michie that Heinemann wanted to publish *The Colossus*, a collection of 48 poems, one-third of which she had written at Yaddo. This was the breakthrough Sylvia had been waiting for for so long in her work. Ted's second collection, *Lupercal*, had already been accepted and was working its way toward publication at Faber and Faber. During this time she also learned that *The London Magazine* was going to publish "The Sleepers" and "Full Fathom Five."

Lupercal was released on March 18 to another set of rave reviews. Ted wanted to celebrate by inviting family and friends to their apartment, but Sylvia, so close to the time she would give birth, was too exhausted to host them. *Lupercal* sold well, which helped the couple financially. They would need all the help they could get with money once they had another mouth to feed in the family.

Finally, on April 1, 1960, little Frieda Rebecca Hughes was born. Sylvia called her mother to tell her the news. She had not labored long—four and one-half hours. Ted was by Sylvia's side during the birth, helping her with his concentration techniques that they had used to relax their minds when they worked. Days before he had hypnotized her and suggested that she have a short, easy delivery. Sylvia had no anesthesia, and Frieda was born healthy—seven pounds, four ounces, and 21 inches long. Sylvia wrote to her mother, "I have never been so happy in my life."[4] The National Health Service in England provided a free midwife to help with the birth and first two weeks of the baby's life. Though she tried to write again just two weeks after Frieda was born, Sylvia was too exhausted from the night feedings to do so. Soon, however, the creative energy of motherhood would show positive effects on her work.

Ted's second book of poems won the Somerset Maugham Award and had elicited more attention and social and work engagements. One of these was an invitation for him and Sylvia on May 4, 1960, to a dinner party at the home of T.S. Eliot. They met Eliot's wife, Valerie, and drank sherry in the living room while Eliot talked about touring the United States. This put Sylvia a bit more at ease. Stephen Spender and his wife, concert pianist Natasha Litvin, were also at the party. Talk moved to gossip about people the Spenders and Eliots knew—names like Stravinsky, Auden, Virginia Woolf, and D.H. Lawrence.

The summer of 1960 began a good period in Plath's work and life. *The New Yorker* published her poem "Watercolor of Grantchester Meadows" and *The London Magazine* printed her short story "The Daughters of Blossom Street." She corrected proofs for *Colossus*. She was working on a new piece as well. That summer she finished "Sleep in the Mohave Desert," "On Deck," and "Two Campers in Cloud Country." *The New Yorker* bought the latter two right away and in August published "The Netmenders."

While Ted's *Lupercal* was being published by Harper in the United States, Plath's collection was turned down for a third time by the Yale Series of Younger Poets. Sylvia could not understand this struggle for a first book in the United States, when her husband, a Brit, had now published two there. She believed her work was superior to the other first books that appeared in the Yale series. In England, however, the BBC, which often featured interviews with writers and poets reading their work on-air, featured her reading "Leaving Early" and "Candles." Finally, in October, Plath enjoyed the publication in England of her first collection, *Colossus*. Sylvia waited to hear the reviews.

She waited longer than she anticipated, and that was a problem. The book did not get much notice, nor generate much buzz. Only three small notices came out over the next two months. Finally, in *The Observer*, A. Alvarez wrote an article titled "The Poet and the Poetess." In it he praised Plath for making no excuses and staying away from "feminine charm, deliciousness, gentility, supersensitivity and the act of being a poetess. She simply writes good poetry." He also admitted that *Colossus* was not without its faults and described "language that goes off on its own," feeling that weakens, and rhetoric that "hovers close to the whimsy of fairy stories."[5] Another review, by John Wain in *The Spectator*, appeared in January 1961. Overall, it was positive, but he found some of the poems too imitative.

Early in 1961, Sylvia found out that she was pregnant again. Her appendix was acting up, and she would have to undergo an appendectomy. The day after they went to a party for Theodore Roethke, the American poet Plath most admired now next to Robert Lowell, she miscarried. She had the appendectomy a brief time afterwards. As she was healing from the miscarriage, Sylvia spent time with Frieda and wrote. Poems she wrote in this period reflected on women's various experiences with bearing or not bearing children and included "Parliament Hill Fields," "Morning Song," "Barren Women," and "Heavy Women." Others from this time included "Face Lift," "Whitsun," and "Zoo Keeper's Wife."

While she was in the hospital recovering from the appendectomy, Ted brought her an airmail letter from *The New Yorker*. They had mailed her a first-reading contract, requesting first refusal on any of her new poems. The contract included various fees that would be paid to her for remaining on this status with them and incorporated additional payment for poems that the magazine decided to publish. With the contract, *The New Yorker* had mailed a check for $100. Sylvia was ecstatic over this boost of confidence in her future work and the promise of future income as a result of it. The idea of sending her work first to them was not a problem; that was something she had been doing automatically for years anyway.

During her continued recovery, Sylvia wrote a poem she first called "Sickroom Tulips in Hospital," then later retitled "Tulips." In the poem, the speaker studies a bouquet of tulips in her hospital room and meditates on their connection to her. The tulips seem to watch her, their redness speaking to the blood of her heart and her wounds. Their vividness warms the room, drawing in all the oxygen to the flowers. They make the ill woman feel even further away from regaining her health.

That spring, Plath corresponded with editors at Alfred A. Knopf about an American publication of *The Colossus*. They wanted sections of "Poem for a Birthday" cut and took other poems Sylvia suggested they include instead. The negotiations continued until it became evident that the American edition was a done deal, just details about the final form it would take were being decided upon. Sylvia was overjoyed to think that she was finally publishing her first book of poetry in America. Boosted by this success, she asked Alfred Kazin to recommend her for a Saxton grant to write a novel.

Perhaps from her time in the hospital for the appendectomy (she had Frieda at home with a midwife), but around this time in the spring of 1961, Sylvia began work on a secret project, a novel about a young woman who has had a nervous breakdown. She was composing it on her typewriter on the back of pink memorandum sheets from Smith College.

In April of that year, she wrote to a friend, she was about a third of the way through the first draft. Because the events were so similar to her own life story, Sylvia did not tell very many people about the project or its contents.

That summer, Aurelia arrived for a visit and to meet her granddaughter. Ted, Sylvia, Frieda, and Aurelia all went to visit Ted's family in Yorkshire. Aurelia got along well with Ted's parents, which pleased Sylvia. The Christmas before, Sylvia had a run-in with Ted's sister, Olwyn, and some of their family times together had turned tense as a result. The feeling was that Olwyn did not like Sylvia and did not accept her as Ted's wife. Sylvia believed Olwyn was jealous of her over the publication of *The Colossus* and Sylvia's intimacy with her brother. She was told that Olwyn did not like her brother Gerald's wife, either. For her part, Olwyn thought Sylvia was not good for Ted. She allegedly saw her as too controlling, possessive, and nagging. Interestingly, the discord between the two women had unexpected but important ramifications in Sylvia's publishing history later on.

COURT GREEN

That summer Ted and Sylvia were hunting for housing. They had been living in a tiny apartment in Chalcot Square, London, and borrowing study space from friends in which to work. Now they wanted something in the countryside, preferably in Devon. They found a house in North Tawton that they liked. North Tawton consisted primarily of one main road with a few shops, pubs, and a few houses. A narrow road led up to the village, and the surrounding countryside was lined with hedgerows and pastures where sheep and cattle grazed peacefully.

Court Green, the property the Hugheses were interested in, consisted of three acres of land and a two-story, 12-room house with a thatched roof. The house had been originally built in the tenth century and had walls three feet thick. Court Green included stables and a two-room servant's cottage near the house. The main house had a cobblestone court. The buildings and property needed heavy repairs. The land contained orchards of 72 apple trees, cherry trees, and bushes of blackberries and raspberries and, to Ted's delight, a prehistoric mound that was possibly a burial ground. Potatoes lay buried in another spot. Court Green was one hour from the coast and 20 minutes from Exeter. A train station with regular trains to London was only a mile away. A graveyard lined one edge of the property.

If the Hugheses moved there, they would be landowners in addition to homeowners and would have to contend with the physical labor that entailed. It would be quite different from their literary lives in London where they had by now become accustomed to going to parties and other events with the intelligentsia and literati of the city and being close to the communications industries of the BBC and publishing houses. Because there was time left on their lease, the Hugheses sublet their London apartment to another couple. The couple who ended up renting it from them were poet David Wevill and his wife, Assia Gutmann. Assia was thought by many to have a beautiful face; David was her third husband. The entrance of the Wevills into the Hugheses' lives would later prove to be a fateful and dramatic one.

On August 31, 1961, Ted and Sylvia moved to Court Green. Sylvia was by then four months pregnant. During their move, Sylvia's brother Warren made his first visit to his sister in England. While there, he helped move furniture (since Sylvia was less able to lift with the new pregnancy following a miscarriage) and make repairs with Ted. Sylvia took Warren to an auction, then on a picnic, and they went to see the Exeter Cathedral together. With having more room, the Hugheses could entertain guests more frequently. After Warren left on September 15, a Portuguese couple they knew from London came to stay for the weekend. With the house being so far out in the country, visitors from London were normally expected to stay the night.

Life at Court Green settled into a fairly regular routine. Sylvia liked writing in the morning, so she would do that while Ted watched little Frieda. Then they would switch, with Sylvia taking care of Frieda in the afternoons. In the evenings, Sylvia usually cooked dinner, and then they relaxed together, often reading. Sylvia's work during that first fall at Court Green included "Wuthering Heights," "Blackberrying," and "The Moon and the Yew Tree." "Blackberrying" came from walking through the blackberry bushes with Warren while he visited and is often regarded as one of Plath's best poems. The latter poem was inspired by a writing assignment given to her by Ted. In one of his concentration exercises, he suggested that she study or think about an object and let her mind free associate to it and away from it. This time, he suggested she do this with a yew tree that stood by their house. Today the poem is often anthologized, as is another popular poem, "Mirror," which she also wrote during this period in Devon. Interestingly, the moon, which was always a favorite image of Plath's, reappears with more frequency again in her work when she moved to the country where the city lights did not interfere with her view of it.

In November 1961, Sylvia was notified by the Eugene F. Saxton Foundation that she had won a $2,000 grant to work on her first novel. Though unknown to them, she actually had completed the novel already; she would send in regular reports on its progress, including chapter outlines, summaries, and page counts as part of the requirements of the grant. In fact, she had already sent the first draft of *The Bell Jar* to James Michie in London in October, who accepted it for Heinemann to publish in England. Because the events in the novel so closely followed her biography of the summer and fall of 1953, Sylvia chose to publish it under a pseudonym, Victoria Lucas.

Interestingly, while she was in London that October for her birthday, Sylvia gave the original manuscript of *The Colossus* to a book dealer to sell. The dealer had recently sold two of Ted's original manuscripts to Indiana University, and now with a house and mortgage and one child with another on the way soon, the couple needed all the money they could get. At that time, though they might have dreamed of it, neither of them could ever have expected the storehouse of manuscripts and papers that would be collected in their names by at least three major colleges in the United States four decades later.

NOTES

1. Qtd. in Diane Middlebrook, *Her Husband: Hughes and Plath—A Marriage* (New York: Viking, 2003), p. 2.

2. Qtd. in Middlebrook, *Her Husband*, p. 3.

3. Sylvia Plath, *The Unabridged Journals of Sylvia Plath, 1950–1962*, ed. Karen V. Kukil (New York: Random House, 2000), pp. 212–13.

4. Sylvia Plath, *Letters Home: Correspondence 1950–1963*, ed. Aurelia Schober Plath (New York: Harper & Row, 1975), p. 374.

5. Qtd. in Paul Alexander, *Rough Magic: A Biography of Sylvia Plath* (New York: Viking Press, 1991), p. 251.

Chapter 6

THE BELL JAR CRACKS
(1962–1963)

Leafing through the pages of Sylvia's 1962 calendar, one would not suspect that it was one of the most important years of her life. The squares of the days are filled with small reminders to wash her hair, buy potatoes, clean or paint, and make appointments related to her work, just like anyone else's calendar would have on it today. Behind the innocent façade of the calendar of days, however, were three important events that occurred that year—the birth of her second child, the breakup of her marriage, and the period of greatest creative achievement and productivity of her life. Some have said perhaps the intensity of the poetry she wrote in October 1962, the sheer drain of it, was what killed her. She lived to see only 43 days of the following year.

Sylvia's labor in January 1962 was not as short as the one she had with Frieda nearly two years earlier. After 18 hours of struggle, a Dr. Webb was summoned and arrived at their country home. It was already too late, however; Nicholas Farrar Hughes appeared on the scene on January 17, just as the doctor arrived. Weighing nine pounds, eleven ounces, Nicholas had dark hair and dark eyes. Sylvia thought he looked a lot like Ted; she was surprised when Ted did not seem to respond the way she expected. Though they had preferred a son when Frieda was born but were delighted with her just the same, Ted did not seem especially pleased to have a boy now.

The beginning of the year into the spring sounds almost idyllic to an outsider looking in on the Hughes household. Though money continued to be tight and Court Green needed constant work and repair, the couple were etching out another working routine for themselves and taking care of their young family. Ted took care of Frieda during the day, so Sylvia could nurse and care for Nicholas for both his night and day feedings. They had help come in for assistance with cleaning. Around the demands of the family, Ted and Sylvia continued to write and submit work to publishers. Ted put in and maintained a vegetable garden, and once she had recovered from childbirth, Sylvia began taking horseback riding lessons at a stable nearby. Court Green's property had massive beds of daffodils that Sylvia and Ted walked through with their children in the spring. They picked from 600 to 1,000 of the sunny yellow flowers and sold them at a local farmer's market. Other flowers on the grounds included roses, gladioli, zinnias, honeysuckle, lilacs, and laburnums.

In April, Sylvia wrote "Little Fugue," a poem about the death of a father. She also wrote "First Appearance," "Crossing the Water," "Pheasant," and "Among the Narcissi." One of her more outstanding poems of this time was "Elm." The poem associates the elm with a woman who has suffered a lost love. It depicts how the power of a lost love can be so strong that it can be destructive. Whether Sylvia sensed a distancing in Ted emotionally during this period is unclear. At the time, there were no external known reasons why she should feel so. However, that was soon to change.

THE BREAK UP

On the weekend of May 19 and 20, 1962, the Hugheses invited the Wevills from their flat in London out to Court Green. They had more visitors now that they lived in larger quarters; Sylvia did most of the preparations and cooking for the Hugheses' company. She looked forward to the arrival of the Wevills more than she did the upcoming planned visit of Ted's family the following month. The Wevills had much in common with the Hugheses. David was a poet, and Assia worked in advertising, but she had an interest in writing poetry herself.

During the weekend, Assia, who was known to flirt openly with men she liked and especially with poets, began to show an interest in Ted. Their glances to one another became more frequent, and a sexual tension seemed to build between them. One account of events tells of Assia finding Ted alone at the kitchen table early one morning drinking coffee. The story goes that she walked over behind him and lifted her nightgown up over his head, enclosing both of them inside of it. Whether this incident occurred or not, apparently by the time the Wevills left, Assia and Ted had secretly arranged to meet in London.

Perhaps Sylvia tried to turn a blind eye to what she sensed happened that weekend. Rather than confront Ted, she poured her doubts into her writing, including new poems "Event" and "The Rabbit Catcher." When the Hughes family visit in June went better than expected (Olwyn did not come, and the family went out to dinner most of the time rather than ask Sylvia to cook), Sylvia wrote to Aurelia that she was enjoying her life. She spent time with her children, in the garden, and reading. Her ambitions for her writing were still strong, but for once she seemed to be able to enjoy the fact that as a couple they had reached a new plateau of notoriety and influence through Ted's work. His children's book was popular, his two books of poems had been reviewed well, and he was now about to publish his first book of collected poems in England. His appearances on the BBC and familiarity with noted poets and writers of the day had boosted his reputation even further. Ted Hughes had reached a position of power within the British literary community, and his star was still rising. The future looked bright for both of them, and money was surely to become less of a problem in the not so distant future.

If Sylvia was finding some satisfaction through her husband's success, she was also coming into her own in terms of her own work. Having children seemed to have given her a quiet confidence in her own abilities that she had always lacked before. Ted was gone more often, and she had the space and countryside in which to work and gain inspiration. Her children seemed to fuel her creativity. When she met A. Alvarez at Court Green, he had the opinion that the balance of power had actually shifted from her husband to herself and that she was about to write some of the best poetry of her life.

That summer Aurelia came to visit at Court Green. Ted and Sylvia had recently been to a local meeting of beekeepers and were beginning to tend to a new box of Italian hybrid bees that had just been delivered and settled some distance from the house. Ted was nursing six bee stings when his mother-in-law from America, the wife of a specialist in bees who had cowritten her husband's book on them, arrived at his home. Sylvia showed her mother around Court Green. Aurelia noticed the decorative painting Sylvia had done on the floor tiles, furniture, and other places. She enjoyed her grandchildren; Frieda became reacquainted with her right away, and Nicholas was content in her arms.

Sylvia told her that she was happy. Her husband was successful; she had two beautiful healthy children, a home she loved and which would be very pleasant one day when they were done working on it, and a career with a bright future. She had started a new novel, a sequel to *The Bell Jar*, in which Ted was the model for the hero; it had a happy ending. It was about a young woman's trip to England, her days there, and her romance and return to America. Still, perhaps with a mother's intuition, Aurelia sensed that all was not quite right. She believed there was a tension of some kind between Sylvia and her husband and that depression lay underneath the surface of everything Sylvia was saying to her.

Her fears bore out when the telephone rang once during Aurelia's stay, and Ted fell down the stairs trying to catch it before Sylvia did. It turned out to be Assia Wevill, who, surprised to hear Sylvia pick up, lowered her voice and tried to sound like a man asking for Ted. Without saying a word, Sylvia handed the phone to Ted, who scrambled up from the floor to take the receiver. After talking a short while, he hung up, and Sylvia walked over to the wall and yanked the telephone cord out of it. Aurelia did not need an interpreter to know what she was witnessing.

Sylvia asked her mother to watch Frieda, and she picked up Nick and ran out of the house and got in the car. She drove off in a rage, first stopping at a friend's house, then driving off again. The friend, Elizabeth Compton, recalled the incident later in vivid detail. She said that Sylvia was hysterical, complaining that her milk had dried up and that she could not feed Nick. Her husband was in love with another woman, she said, Assia Wevill, and Sylvia was scared of her. She told Elizabeth that her husband had become a little man, that she had given him her whole heart and it could never now come back. It was gone forever.

To ease the awkwardness, Aurelia decided to stay with the Hugheses' friend Winifred Davies when Sylvia came back the next morning. She came each day to watch the children so Ted and Sylvia could work or talk. Sylvia wrote what she could, including a poem naked in its account of current events, "Words Heard, by Accident, over the Phone." One evening, though, she could not contain her rage through her work and built a fire outside where they normally burned their trash. With Aurelia looking on, she tore pages of her new novel, the happy sequel to *The Bell Jar*, and threw it piece by piece into the open flames. The novel, which was once going to be a birthday present to her husband, would never be completed.

It was bad enough that her marriage was falling apart, but for it to happen in front of her mother's eyes must have been especially excruciating for Sylvia, who had always tried so hard to please her mother and whose relationship with her had been so intertwined with the time of her previous emotional breakdown. Aurelia had been with her when she faced the rejection of Frank O'Connor over the Harvard Summer School class, and she was with her now.

Before long, she had another episode of anger at the bonfire where she burned all of her letters from her mother. This was particularly painful for Aurelia, who hoped one day they could publish their correspondence.

Aurelia, of course, still had all of Sylvia's letters to her, which she did publish in *Letters Home* some years later. However, her own efforts at writing, so little of which had ever been acknowledged in her lifetime and could have been published with her daughter's in a collection, were now gone forever out of Sylvia's emotional episode. A more understandable but equally tragic third exorcism at the bonfire occurred still later when Sylvia took many of Ted's papers, letters, poems, and drafts and threw them into the raging flames as well.

Aurelia left on August 4, as originally planned. By August 27, she received a letter from Sylvia notifying her that she was planning to get a legal separation from Ted. She did not want a divorce because she did not believe in it; she simply could go on no longer living a lie and being treated this way by Ted. By now, he was staying in London during the week, returning to Devon only on weekends. Sylvia wrote that she felt especially bad for her children. She knew what it was like to grow up without a father, and now her own children were doomed to repeat the experience. At least the legal separation, she believed, would force Ted to pay child support and not spend all of their money maintaining a separate life in London.

Late in August, the Hugheses' friends the Comptons offered Sylvia emotional support. Sylvia, as was her normal pattern, became ill from the stress of the summer's events; she got the flu. She was driving a car one day and suddenly swerved off the road into an abandoned airfield. Concerned people afterwards claimed that it was a sign of Sylvia's potential to hurt herself. In a last-ditch effort to save her marriage, she talked Ted into going to Ireland that September, where she thought they might be able to talk things out away from the watchful eye of people they both knew. Ted went along with the plan, and they began to talk about where in Ireland they might like to go. Friends would take care of Frieda and Nicholas.

Taking the train on September 11, the Hugheses headed off for Ireland. They arrived in Dublin, where they enjoyed oysters, brown bread, and Guinness. From there they went to Galway, and from there north along the Connemara to Cleggan, where poet Richard Murphy lived. Murphy took them out on his boat, the *Ave Maria*, to Inishbofin to see the tower of W. B. Yeats. Climbing to the top, Sylvia felt a spiritual connection to the poet. She had been associating herself with Yeats quite a lot in her mind before this, so the moment had special meaning for her.

In fact, the Hugheses seemed to be looking for signs. One evening, Ted got out the Ouija board to demonstrate its powers to Murphy, but Murphy was not interested, and Sylvia left Ted to work whatever magic he thought it had with Irish poet Thomas Kinsella, who had come by to visit.

Walking along a hallway in Murphy's house, Ted thought he saw a portrait on the wall change. Ted read this as a sign that it was time for him to leave. Without telling Sylvia where he was going, he simply packed up his things and was gone.

Stunned that he should do such a thing when they were trying to reconcile, Sylvia left soon afterwards. When she arrived back home at Court Green, she found a telegram from Dr. Barnhouse waiting for her. It instructed her that for her own health she not play into Ted's immaturity or disloyalty and wait for him to grow out of it but that she demand a divorce from him immediately and make a clean break. On September 25, 1962, Sylvia went into London to speak with a lawyer. The next day, she wrote the poem, "For a Fatherless Son." When Ted appeared unannounced in late September at Court Green, presumably to remove his things, Sylvia was outraged and told him to leave immediately. He would have to find another time to take care of his belongings.

The separation became more real to her and her plans more set in motion when she began telling other people about what she was going to do and when she began writing her poetry again, in spite of it all. She wrote about the break up to Olive Higgins Prouty in late September. She wrote to her mother that she could not come back to America or see her until she had managed to create a new life for herself. She told her not to send the money that she had offered; Ted would be paying enough to support the house and children, and she could make enough from her writing to cover her own needs. She wrote the poem, "The Birthday Present" and resolved to begin the task of the important writing she needed to do to help support herself and her children immediately.

ARIEL AND OCTOBER 1962

On the morning of October 1, 1962, Sylvia woke around 4 o'clock in the morning, took her coffee, and went into her study at Court Green where she worked for several hours until the children rose around eight. She worked this way for the next few weeks, beginning a series of poems that would change her reputation and legacy in American literature. The first poem she wrote that October was "The Detective." The next was "The Courage of Shutting-up." She dated each poem as she completed it, stacked it on a growing pile, and took up another sheet of pink Smith memorandum paper. The next ones were a series of five poems about bees: "The Bee Meeting," "The Arrival of the Bee Box," "Stings," "The Swarm," and "Wintering." On October 10, she wrote "A Secret" and on the 11th, "The Applicant." Out of pain and indignation, Sylvia was writing astounding poems at a fast and continuous rate, the best poems she had ever written in her life.

On October 12, she returned to her lifelong complications with her father's death and plunged headlong through them with the composition of "Daddy." The poem is terrifying to many readers, some of whom do not understand its references to the father as a German Nazi. Sylvia was combining images of her father, her husband, and perhaps other male figures at whom she had been angry over a lifetime together in the image of the father in the poem. When the speaker says she is through with Daddy at the end of the poem, Sylvia seems to have worked her way through, and become done with, all of these male-dominating forces that had frustrated her for so long.

On October 16, she wrote "Medusa" and on the 17th, "The Jailer." Perhaps it was no accident that Sylvia was composing these poems on the backs of the pink memorandum stationery from Smith on which she had also drafted *The Bell Jar*. Some were written on the back of a draft of Ted's abandoned play, *The Calm*. Sylvia's handwriting, so schoolmarmish and legible in her journals and elsewhere before this time, becomes ferocity in black ink in the drafts of these October poems, driving and erratic squiggles on the pages. She is clearly writing them with determination and great emotion, but with a control of the language that she had never before been able to master. Even visually on the pages of her drafts, the poems are different. At this same time she wrote to her mother, "I am a writer...I am a genius of a writer; I have it in me. I am writing the best poems of my life; they will make my name."[1]

"Stopped Dead" was composed on October 19 and "Fever 103°" on the 20th. On October 21, Plath wrote "Amnesiac" and "Lyonnesse." On the 24th, she wrote "Cut" and "By Candlelight." On her 30th birthday, the first without Ted, she wrote "Poppies in October" and "Ariel." Ariel was the name of the horse Sylvia was learning to ride that year. Though local people said there was nothing particularly noteworthy about the horse itself, it was clear that Sylvia's growing confidence in riding became linked in her imagination with her growing power as a poet and an independent woman. The poem is a celebration of female strength and power and echoes back to the Ariel in Shakespeare's *The Tempest* that she saw with her mother and Warren in Boston when she was a girl. In "Ariel's Song" from that play, a father's body lies under the sea where it is refashioned by the movement of the water into something beautiful and lasting. For all that the father and the ocean came to represent to Plath, this collection seemed to be doing the same. The poem and title held such meaning for her that she would decide to use it as the title poem for the entire collection.

On October 28, she wrote "Purdah" and "Nick and the Candlestick" and finished a poem she had begun earlier, "Lady Lazarus." The latter poem has become one closely associated with Plath's life. The speaker is a 30-year-old woman who tries to commit suicide as a means to mark each decade. Not long after these poems were written, Plath went to London to record several of her new poems for the BBC. These recordings still exist and are haunting to many listeners.

Plath's deep, rich, cultured New England voice on the BBC recordings of the *Ariel* poems speaks clearly and forcefully. Her voice sounds older than her 30 years. She sounds like someone who has lived through a lot in the writing of these poems; her voice takes on even greater conviction and strength in the power of the language. Still, a voice that confident and full of rage can be frightening and unnerving for listeners, especially when it is disembodied through hearing it in a recording. The voice expresses controlled rage, anger pent up at men, society, her mother, her father, and anyone who never understood her or who thought her work not worthy of their attention. She is angry at a world that would not allow women to write and be mothers and wives and homemakers, and she is angry at how perhaps none of these roles can ever be quite reached at the level of perfection she once dreamed possible.

WINTER IN LONDON

Sylvia returned to London on November 5 to look for an apartment so that she could be closer to publishers and other sources of her work until she could get a foothold with some steady money. She planned to go back to Devon in the spring. Staying involved financially and also in particular in caring for Frieda, Ted helped her look for a flat that they could afford. On their first trip out, they found nothing of any consequence. The next time, Sylvia went out walking by herself and came upon a sign that an apartment was for rent at 23 Fitzroy Road. It turned out there were two apartments available in the building, an upper and a lower. The upper consisted of three bedrooms on an upper level and a bath, kitchen, and living room on a lower level. It even had a balcony for taking in the sun once spring arrived. Sylvia thought it was perfect. The best part, however, was the plaque that the building had affixed to the outside. The plaque read, "William Butler Yeats 1865–1939 Irish Poet and Dramatist Lived Here." She wrote to her mother that that was all the sign she needed that this was the place for her to live with the children in London. Living there would bless her work.

She put in an offer right away, but because of a procedure of checking references and other paperwork, she had to wait to learn if the apartment could be hers. Back at Court Green to wait, she took yet another stock of her poetry collection, this time especially the most recent grouping that she had written in such a blitz. She had always envisioned this group as a book. What to title the book became a question for awhile. She decided she would dedicate its British publication to Frieda and Nicholas and its American publication to Olive Higgins Prouty. She discarded titles such as *Daddy and Other Poems* and *The Rival and Other Poems*. *Ariel and Other Poems* settled in as the choice that would stick.

Per her arrangement with *The New Yorker*, Sylvia sent editor Howard Moss almost every poem from *Ariel*. To her great surprise and disappointment, Moss accepted only "Amnesiac." She sent several to *The Atlantic Monthly*, but they only purchased "The Arrival of the Bee Box" and "Wintering," rejecting nearly a dozen others. Even the smaller literary journals did not accept the *Ariel* poems. Sylvia was beginning to wonder whether they were too personal and would not be published at all. Though she continued to believe in their quality, the self-doubt about her talent began stomping around in her thoughts once again. Despite these doubts, she continued to write. In November, she wrote "Years," "The Fearful," "Mary's Song," and "Winter Trees."

It was Thanksgiving time, and still Sylvia had not heard any news about the apartment in London. Another applicant for the space, an artist named Trevor Thomas, had put in his bid before Sylvia, but his payment and paperwork were so far unsatisfactory. Sylvia checked on the matter and made another offer. She was willing to sign a five-year lease, pay the entire first year in advance, and send a reference of her mother, Professor A.S. Plath from America. This was enough to seal the deal, and a moving-in date of December 17 was set. Thomas would take the downstairs flat.

Though her work and living arrangements appeared to suggest Plath was dealing with things since Ted left, Aurelia and the rest of the family back home in America were not so sure. Aurelia plagued her with letters, asking about her welfare, the welfare of the children, about her finances, and especially about her health. Sylvia's letters went from reassuring and confident to whining to desperate as she detailed for her mother and her aunt and others her shifting moods and details about how things were going. The biggest problem she complained about in Ted's absence was not missing him but the gap in affordable, dependable, and quality childcare while she worked that his leaving had caused. Nannies were hard to come by in Devon, and the ones who were available either did not get along with Sylvia or did not work out for some other reason.

Aurelia was beside herself with worry, though she respected her daughter's wishes and did not go back to England. She sent money; she called doctors and mother's helpers to try and help or look after her. Aunt Dot, Aurelia's sister, sent Sylvia all of her life's savings from before her marriage. She had put the money away when she got married to use some day for something very special. When she sent the money to Sylvia as a gift, explaining to her that she thought this was the something she thought to be that special, giving Sylvia a new start when she needed it, the poet burst into tears. The $700 was just what she needed to help get herself settled in her new London flat. With it she intended to buy a new gas stove, straw mats, and other furnishings.

Also during November, Sylvia learned that *The Bell Jar* had been turned down by Knopf in America. Aurelia would later claim that her daughter did not want it published there, that she had written it quickly for money and only wanted it to appear in Great Britain. Still, Sylvia was glad to hear that Heinemann planned to send it out to other houses in the States. In early December, she finished "Ocean 1212-W," a memoir about her grandparents that uses their telephone number in Winthrop as its title. She had also started a new novel. *Doubletake,* or *Double Exposure,* as she later renamed it, was a story about a woman who discovers her husband is an adulterer.

On December 10, 1962, Sylvia moved with Frieda and Nicholas into the 23 Fitzroy Road apartment in London. When she arrived, the new stove had not yet been installed. When she went inside and came back out, the wind slammed the door behind her and locked her keys inside. The gas men arrived with the stove and had to crawl in over the back roof and break a window to get in. She still waited for a telephone. The electricity was not turned on either, and the movers had to unload her belongings that night by candlelight. If Yeats's previous presence in the flat was supposed to bless her work, it was apparently not helping with the practical matters of light and cooking. Eerily, as would be seen in just two months, the family may have been better off had Aunt Dot's gift money not been used to purchase the stove in the first place.

With Sylvia and the children back in London, Ted came by more frequently to see them. The relative peace Sylvia had found to write in Devon was destroyed in London with this constant stirring up of old feelings. Once, Ted took them all to the London Zoo, and during the outing Sylvia became furious with him. She often visited A. Alvarez, the writer who had written the first serious review of *The Colossus* and had been a steady fan. She read him more of her new poems and hinted at wanting to begin a romantic relationship with him. Alvarez had at one time also tried to commit suicide, so Sylvia discussed this with him. He wrote later that she had been going over the proofs of *The Bell Jar* and was most likely reliving the experience in her mind as she did so. Also, the abandonment she had felt after her father died was reenacting itself in the rejection by Ted. Alvarez feared for Sylvia and encouraged her work during her visits. Though he was seeing another woman romantically, he tried to be there for her as a friend.

By Christmas, Sylvia had done much to decorate the apartment. She painted the walls white, covered the floors with mats, installed pine bookshelves, and bought a small glass-topped table. Though the apartment looked better, it still did not appear homelike to many of the visitors who saw it. The Christmas holidays themselves were miserable to think of for her and the children without friends or family, so Sylvia called some friends, and they were invited to their homes at different times over the holidays. When she invited A. Alvarez over for Christmas evening, Alvarez knew that she wanted more than the companionship of a friend. He went for drinks and left when she accosted him with the desire to have an affair. He knew she was desperate and vulnerable, and he was not sufficiently safe from his own depression to deal with hers besides. She took his level-headed kindness on both of their behalfs as another rejection and never called or saw him again.

LAST DAYS, 1963

January 1963 in London was a terribly cold one, the coldest, it was said, in over 100 years. Londoners all over the city struggled to keep warm and healthy and to have enough energy to cook their meals and enough light to see at night. Sylvia's was not the only apartment where the heat went off, pipes froze, and the electricity kept coming on and going off, but this happened often enough in her flat that both children were ill with colds, and she suffered with flu and raging headaches of sinusitis. What's more, her telephone had still not been installed, so whenever she absolutely needed to make a call, she had to go out in the subzero temperatures and make a call from a pay phone. The children, too young to understand what had happened, reacted to their parents' break up by having emotional upsets when Ted came to visit, only to leave again.

That month, *The Bell Jar* was released in England, under its pseudonym, Victoria Lucas. Reviews were good. Robert Taubman called it "the first feminine novel I've read in the Salinger mode."[2] Perhaps encouraged by the reviews, Sylvia began writing poetry again at the end of January after several weeks off. She wrote "Sheep in Fog," "Child," "Totem," "The Munich Mannequins," "Paralytic," and "Gigolo." On February 1, she wrote "Mystic," "Kindness," and "Words." On February 4, she wrote two more poems, "Balloons," and "Edge." "Edge" describes a woman who is only "perfected" through suicide.

People who knew Sylvia and her circumstance tried to help with her illness and depression, but no one was available all of the time. She still struggled to find childcare so that she could work; she was taking sleeping pills to try to get enough rest; Ted was in and out of hers and the children's lives keeping them stirred up, yet also providing the child support they needed; her mother wrote (she could not call with Sylvia not having a phone); and friends took turns making sure she was taking her depression medications and seeing her psychiatrist. There seemed to be a growing sense of danger about Sylvia, prompted in some cases by erratic behavior. When Ted came to visit, he usually came from the same direction down the street. Observers said they would see Sylvia watching in the window for longer and longer intervals in that direction for him to appear.

Trevor Thomas in the apartment downstairs had an unexpected visit from his neighbor one evening. Announcing that she was Sylvia Plath, she opened his newspaper and showed him a poem of Ted's there and then turned to a review of *The Bell Jar* and pointed to that saying she was its au- thor. Thomas had never put the two together before to realize who Mrs. Hughes was. She told him she was going to die, and she wondered who would take care of her children. On February 4, she wrote to her mother, "I have been feeling a bit grim—the upheaval over, I am seeing the final- ity of it all, and being catapulted from the cowlike happiness of maternity into loneliness and grim problems is no fun."[3]

Later, Ted Hughes claimed that the two were discussing reconciliation, especially when he had seen how well she had done without him in Devon and then early on in establishing herself back in London. By Jan- uary, he could see that she had been ill and depressed, and he was trying to suggest that they go away together to work on their relationship. How- ever, Sylvia was hot and cold in her response to his advances. He saw her on Thursday, February 7, and again approached her about going away. In- stead, she rebuffed him saying that she had plans for the weekend and would not tell him what they were. Jealousy and mistrust were still highly at play, even as it seems she could not give up on the possibility that she still loved Ted and there might be a hope that they could reconcile.[4]

That weekend, Sylvia took Frieda and Nick with her to Jillian and Gerry Becker's house, two of her newer friends in London. The Beckers knew enough about Sylvia's situation, history, and treatments with her psychiatrist, Dr. Horder, to know that she should not be left alone, that she had reached a serious stage in her depression. In *Giving Up: The Last Days of Sylvia Plath: A Memoir*, Jillian Becker describes that Sylvia called her from a pay phone about 2 o'clock in the afternoon on Thursday, February 7, and asked if she could come over with the children. When she got there, she said she felt terrible and immediately asked to go to bed. About 4, she came out and told Jillian that she did not want to go home and asked if she would go by Fitzroy Road and retrieve overnight clothes, toothbrushes, and a change of clothes for the morning for her and her children. Oddly, she asked Jillian to find a certain fancy dress of hers in the closet. She also asked for two books, *The Ha-Ha* by Jennifer Dawson and *Escape from Freedom* by Erich Fromm.

Jillian took the key and went to the apartment. There she found the dress and the baby's things, but she could not find a change of clothes for Frieda. Jillian had daughters, so she decided they could adapt something she had at home for her. When she reached the top of the stairs, she saw a sign that said "Quiet! Genius at Work" on the door of Sylvia's tiny study. There was very little of anything on her desk; it was tidy—some paper, pens, and one of the books Sylvia had asked for lay there.

Sylvia ate well at Jillian's, and Jillian was hopeful that this would help Sylvia get well. Unfortunately, her nights were terrible. After giving Jillian her pills and telling her how many she needed and at what intervals, she went to bed early and asked Jillian to sit beside her. She talked and talked, of Ted, Assia Wevill, of getting the children out of London and visiting the sea. Finally, she fell asleep, and Jillian went to bed. Then, in the night Nick woke up, and he woke Frieda. Jillian took the children to Sylvia, and they got them both back to sleep. Jillian went back to bed. Not long later, Sylvia called for her and asked if it were close enough to morning for her to take her wake-up pills yet. It was not. Sylvia told her that the early hours of the morning were the worst for her. As Jillian sat by her, she went back to sleep again.

In the morning, Sylvia ate a good breakfast and took her medicine. Dr. Horder, who was the father of Jillian's daughter's best school friend, called to see how she was. He urged her to make sure Sylvia took her pills morning and evening and that she stayed engaged with the children. It was important that she remember how vital she was to them, he said. Jillian understood. Try as she might, however, it was getting increasingly more difficult to keep Sylvia engaged. She did not feed her children, wash them, or tend to their diapers. Rather than let it go undone and the children remain uncared for, Jillian wrote later that she did it for her. Finally, one time as Sylvia sat watching Jillian change a dirty diaper of Nick's, she relented and said that she would do it, but by then Jillian had already nearly finished the task.

Saturday night, Jillian claims Sylvia either packed or put on the fancy dress she had asked for and went out, not telling the Beckers where she was going. Jillian suggests in her book that people have told her over the years that Sylvia saw Ted that night, but Ted's account conflicts with this. Jillian does not remember what time Sylvia returned or what mood she was in when she did, but she does recall that Sylvia slept well that night and did not call for her, or if she did Jillian did not hear her.

At brunch on Sunday, Sylvia ate well again. She seemed more relaxed, Jillian thought, from what must have happened or who she saw the night before. They all took a Sunday afternoon nap, and when she emerged for tea, Sylvia said she had slept deeply and well. Relaxed conversation continued about no subjects in particular. There was nothing immediately preceding what happened next, Jillian says, that would indicate Sylvia would ask to go home.

She began packing up hers and the children's things quite suddenly and said that they must get home that evening. She had many things to do, she said, and it appeared to Jillian that Sylvia seemed to think it was somehow urgent to do them. It occurred to Jillian that perhaps Sylvia was feeling better and had just realized that she had a lot to do. She asked her if she would remember to take her medicine; Sylvia stopped her packing to look her in the eye and promised that she would.

Gerry took Sylvia and the children home in an old cab he had for a car. Outside the apartment, he heard her crying through the open window between the seats and went and sat with her in the backseat. Her head was in her hands, and the children were beginning to cry, too. Gerry tried several times to get her to come back to their house with him. He assured her that Jillian did not need for her to leave, and that they would be glad to have her. Sylvia refused. He tried again, and several times again to get her to come back. She kept insisting that she had work to do and that a nurse was coming first thing in the morning. She would take her pills. Gerry walked her and the children upstairs, helping them with their things, telling her again that if she needed anything at all, she could call on them or come back to stay with them. Then he went home; it was about 7 o'clock in the evening.

After he left, Sylvia fed the children and put them to bed. Dr. Horder came by to check on her. Late Sunday night, about 11:45, Sylvia went downstairs to her neighbor Trevor Thomas and asked him for a postage stamp to send mail to America; she wanted to take the mail to the box that night. She seemed groggy and drugged to him; he thought she was ill. When she asked him how much she owed him for the postage, he said she need not bother, but she responded that she wanted to pay or else her conscience would not be clear before God. Also out of the blue, she asked him what time he left for work in the morning. Thomas said 8:30 A.M. After he closed the door, he could tell by the light in the hallway that Sylvia was still there. He opened it and asked if anything was the matter and if he should call Dr. Horder. She said no; she was having a dream, that's all, seeing a wonderful vision. He later reported hearing her pacing the floor upstairs much of the night.

Probably Sylvia never took her pills on the morning of Monday, February 11, 1963. Instead, in those wee hours of the morning that she said were so difficult for her during her spells of depression, she proceeded with the same kind of deliberation she had ten years earlier on that summer afternoon at 26 Elmwood Road in Wellesley. She went to the kitchen and poured her children some milk and prepared them bread, which she took upstairs to their room and set near their beds. Then she opened their window wide open. She closed the door of their room, and with masking tape, she sealed the cracks around it and pressed towels along the bottom. On a piece of shelf paper, she wrote the number of their doctor in two different pens. Apparently, she had to hunt for the number and come back to complete it. She taped this piece of paper to a stroller in the room beside theirs and went back downstairs.

She wrote a note to please call Dr. Horder with the number and went downstairs to the main entryway to the apartment and taped it to the baby carriage. Then she went back up to the kitchen. There she covered the cracks in the windows and doors with towels and clothing. She turned the new gas oven she had purchased with her Aunt Dot's life savings on high. Similar to taking the blanket with her into the crawlspace under her mother's house, that morning she knelt down, folded a towel under her cheek and lay her head deep into the oven. The oven did not get hot, but soon the gas filled the chamber and fumes radiated out into the room.

Nurse Myra Norris arrived at 23 Fitzroy Road at her appointed time of 9:00 A.M. There was no name on the downstairs doorbells, so she was not sure which apartment was that of Sylvia Plath Hughes. She rang Trevor Thomas's bell, but he did not answer. Finally, she walked around the building and saw two children crying at an open window upstairs.

Quickly Nurse Norris solicited the help of a workman down the street, Charles Langridge, and the two of them worked their way into the building. Once inside, they could smell gas coming from the door to the upstairs apartment. Quickly they forced the door and ran upstairs to the kitchen. When they got there, they found Sylvia's body sprawled out on the floor; her head was still in the oven.

They turned off the gas and opened the windows and carried Sylvia into the living room, where Nurse Norris attempted to revive her with artificial respiration. Langridge called the police, then saw the note taped downstairs on the baby carriage to call Dr. Horder, which he did. When Horder arrived, he agreed with Myra Norris, who had stopped her efforts to revive Sylvia, that it was too late. He pronounced her dead at 10:30 A.M. An ambulance arrived and took her body to University College Hospital on Gower Street in Pancras. She was listed as dead on arrival. The cause of death was recorded as carbon monoxide poisoning, a suicide, from depression.

Though both children survived, Trevor Thomas downstairs almost did not. The gas from upstairs had made its way downstairs into his apartment and knocked him unconscious while he slept. He woke up late in the afternoon feeling extremely ill and disoriented. Dr. Horder saw him later and diagnosed him as having carbon monoxide poisoning.

When Sylvia's body had been removed, Dr. Horder phoned Jillian Becker, who took the children and tried to notify Ted Hughes. Becker did not have a number for Ted, so she called another friend who reached him in Soho. On February 12, Ted cabled Sylvia's Aunt Dot, saying simply that Sylvia had died the day before. Ted set about making plans for the funeral. Warren and his wife came to England, but Aurelia was too distraught to make the trip. After a brief inquest into the sudden death was satisfied by the court, the small funeral party went with the body to Yorkshire. Ted wanted his wife to be buried in his family's cemetery on the moors. There in the Hughes family church, a short service was held, and the mourners went to the gravesite.

Later, a gravestone was placed at the site that gave Sylvia's name as Sylvia Plath Hughes and her birth and death dates. As an inscription, Ted chose lines from *Bhagavad Gita,* "Even amidst fierce flames the golden lotus can be planted."[4]

NOTES

1. Sylvia Plath, *Letters Home: Correspondence 1950–1963,* ed. Aurelia Schober Plath (New York: Harper & Row, 1975), p. 468.

2. Qtd. in Paul Alexander, *Rough Magic: A Biography of Sylvia Plath* (New York: Viking Press, 1991), p. 321.

3. Plath, *Letters Home,* p. 498.

4. Qtd. in Alexander, *Rough Magic,* p. 332.

Chapter 7

AFTER PLATH: MYSTERIES AND CONTROVERSIES

Sylvia Plath's untimely death, like other artists and well-known people from the same cause, immediately shrouded her life story in a shadow of mystery. Mysteries and unanswered and unanswerable questions often lead to speculation and rumor, myths and legends, and this has been the case with this mid-twentieth century American poet. Some of these include who or what is to blame for why she killed herself, what has happened to her work after her death, and which stories about her life are true and which are not. Also, the ranking of Plath as a poet regardless of the shroud of her biography and mysterious, dramatic end, remains under some measure of debate.

THE BLAME GAME

When someone commits suicide, family and friends normally go through a period of looking for someone to blame, even considering themselves in a cold, hard light with as much scrutiny as they can stand. "What if?" questions plague the nights of loved ones and friends. What if I had telephoned her that morning? What if I had visited her more often? What if? What if? When a talented, well-known person, someone who appears to "have it all," commits suicide, the blame game expands to include gossip and rumors about likely suspects in the person's life whom the people doing the judging often do not know or do not know well. It also expands to include society at large or the toll of the creative process—the price of digging deep to the darker regions of the human condition and bringing up the truth that one finds there. Surely, a gifted, talented woman would be smart enough not to take her own life. There has to be a good reason to drive one so smart and talented to commit such an act.

Candidates for the winner of the blame game in Sylvia Plath's story have included the poet herself for being, it is said, so self-centered, ambitious, possessive, and high-strung; Ted Hughes for leaving his wife with two small children after she helped him establish his career; Otto Plath for remaining an aloof father both in life as well as in death; and Aurelia Plath for being a mother who pushed her daughter to succeed so that she could live the life of a writer vicariously through her. Society, and the expectations it placed on women in the 1950s, has been another popular reason given for why Sylvia Plath "gave up." Though others have tried to explain suicide as the result of mental illness and emotional disturbance in a more clinical way before, it is only more recently, with the increased understanding and acceptance of mental illness as a disease, that the blame game for suicide has become understood as a futile one. In fact, depression can run in families and has many other sources as well. Otto's estranged family, principally women on his mother's side, had strains of it back in Germany. Depression itself is what drives people over the edge—not people or circumstances; they are merely triggers of depressive episodes in a person who is susceptible to reacting in dangerous ways to things that happen to other people every day.

Those who argue that Sylvia killed herself and no one else is to blame see a woman who was competitive and ambitious. They read her voluminous journals that reveal so little consideration of anyone else or their feelings and concentrate so pointedly and obsessively on her desire to become a great writer. Her journals indicate that above all else she desired to be considered the best. She thinks herself capable of being the Poetess of America. Among female poets in history she considers rivals, she lists no less talents than Sappho, Elizabeth Barrett Browning, Christina Rossetti, Amy Lowell, Emily Dickinson, and Edna St. Vincent Millay. Among the living of her day she sees worthy rivals in Edith Sitwell, Marianne Moore, May Swenson, Isabella Gardner, and Adrienne Rich. With ambition such as this, observers argue, Plath set herself up for a fatalistic blow. Even her beloved high school teacher, Wilbury Crockett, who encouraged her work for three straight school years, said after Sylvia's death that he knew that she was doomed. He said he was saddened but not shocked by what happened.

The history of Ted Hughes before and after his first wife's death did not help his case among the players of the blame game. He cheated on her with Assia Wevill when she was home with a newborn baby and another child of two. From the journals, observers know that two factors always plagued Sylvia's fears—rejection and the fear domestic life would threaten her ability to work and create. Through Ted's betrayal and their separation, Sylvia suffered both at once. Her continuing effort to find help with the children through the immediate aftermath of these events has often struck people as selfish—she worked at home, after all, and apparently did not have to be overly concerned about money as long as she remained frugal. Women today who are employed in work that is meaningful to them understand the continuing struggle between demands of work and family in light of a society that expects them, and now finally men as well, to handle both with aplomb. Hughes paid support, but the children remained under Sylvia's care. It is clear from her letters that when she had help with the children so that she could work, she was less frustrated.

Hughes did not help his case in the blame game either by being associated with another female suicide—Assia Wevill. Wevill not only committed suicide herself a few years later, but also took with her the young daughter she had with Ted. Observers were quick to blame him for this suicide as well—the man must be some kind of woman-killer to have driven two of them so far over the edge in so relatively short a time! While one is tempted to say that this coincidence surely must be more than bad luck, issues that draw people together are complex and complicated. It is more likely that something in Hughes attracted two women with similar illnesses and proclivities, and something in Hughes found both women attractive yet perhaps also contributed to their respective illnesses. If one is looking for blame, perhaps it is surprising that Hughes cannot be blamed for his own death, after suffering the suicide guilt of two women he loved.

Otto Plath, who died when Sylvia was just eight years old, remained a colossal figure in her life and work, long after he was gone. As the old bachelor figure the family lived around when he was home, staying upstairs to give him peace and quiet and coming downstairs only with performances to entertain him, Sylvia apparently rose to the challenge of trying to be perfect in his eyes to win his acceptance and love. Many observers blame Otto's aloofness for setting Sylvia off on a suicide mission of working hard to please others, working even harder to please herself. Her perfectionism is what killed her, these accusers lament, and this perfectionism was set in motion by her father.

Others look back at the poet's background again and see Aurelia repressing her desire to be a writer when she gave in to her father and attended vocational school. They see Aurelia giving in again when she quit her teaching job and stayed home at Otto's request to be a full-time homemaker. They see her taking control after Otto's death and making sure she sent her children to the finest schools in the United States, even though her salary and social position as a widow did not warrant or provide the expectation for such a goal. Was she not overly ambitious for her children?

Transcripts of therapy sessions show that Sylvia had to work through feelings of hatred for her mother that she did not feel she could express when she knew her mother worked so hard to give her opportunities. Observers say that her mother pushed her to succeed, that anything less than success would risk not only losing her love but would also show ingratitude for her mother's sacrifice. Mrs. Plath, like so many mothers, kept all of her daughter's awards and publications and was proud to show them and speak about them, even after her daughter's death. She defended herself when attacked for her relationship with her daughter by publishing *Letters Home*. In that book, readers see Sylvia putting a good face on almost any situation she writes about to her mother. They also read notes inserted by Aurelia, showing efforts made by the family to help Sylvia when Ted left her and to bring her back to America. On the other hand, it was Aurelia who blocked *The Bell Jar* from publication in the United States for fear of libel, claiming that Sylvia wrote the "potboiler" purely for money and would not have wanted it published in the United States. What if she had allowed the children to grieve when their father died? What if she had taken them to the funeral, or at least to the grave, and not made the choice that this would be too much for them to handle, that the best thing to do was to move on and deal with the present and the future as soon as possible? What if she had notified Sylvia's doctors about what she learned in regard to the family history of depression on Otto's side? What if she had gone to London in 1963 regardless of Sylvia's protests?

The blame game and its what ifs about suicide can be endless unless one comes to terms that the game is futile. Suicide is a deadly and unfortunate potential outcome of depression, just as death is an unfortunate potential outcome of alcoholism or cancer or heart disease. Depression itself, not people or circumstances, killed Sylvia Plath.

EDITING CONTROVERSIES

Ted Hughes exacerbated the blame game's cards against him as well by the choices he made in editing his wife's work for posthumous publication. Under British law, even though the couple was separated at the time of Plath's death, Hughes became executor of all of her literary property, and at his death, the rights would go to their children. If the British poet laureate should not be blamed for Plath's death due to suicide, he can be more certainly held accountable as a professional writer and editor about the decisions he made regarding her literary property and legacy after her death. On the one hand, few people would remember Sylvia Plath had Hughes not spent time going through her poems and journals and releasing them in various posthumous editions. The abridged journals were first published in 1982 and edited by Frances McCullough. The *Collected Poems* were published in 1981 and went on to win the Pulitzer Prize. Attempting to walk the fine line between publishing good writing that should be shared with the world and keeping a private personal history from the scrutiny of a curious public for the sake of the couple's young children could not have been easy for Hughes. Over the years certain of Hughes's professional and personal decisions in regard to his wife's work drew more criticism than others from the literary community and the readership at large. Though Hughes could do nothing right in the view of some circles, the bulk of the questions arose out of the publication of the poet's last poetry collection, *Ariel*, as well as the journals.

Ariel first appeared in 1966, three years after the poet's death. Instead of publishing all of the original poems in the order in which Plath left them, Hughes left out some poems, included others, and rearranged the rest. Though Hughes argued the aesthetic reasoning behind his editorial decisions, his work was regarded as heavy-handed, manipulative, and intrusive. This was all the more the case since a large number of the poems in *Ariel* were written in October 1962, during Plath's burst of creative energy that occurred after their separation, and the others were written weeks and days before her death. That the man who betrayed her and whom they believed tripped her final breakdown should also have such a heavy hand in altering her work and legacy after her death was too much for some readers to stand. The case against Hughes began to grow to nearly warlike proportions.

Edited by Frances McCullough, a friend of Hughes, *The Journals of Sylvia Plath* that were published in 1982 drew the ire of feminist critics almost immediately. The journals were incomplete and fueled as much mystery about the poet as they clarified. Hughes claimed that he "lost" one notebook and destroyed the very last one, the journal written up to days before his wife's death, out of protection for the children. Feminists cried foul, saying that Hughes was protecting himself from damaging personal information the journals must have contained about him. Plath had recently separated from him, and her letters were filled with anger, jealousy, and frustration over their relationship while at the same time she was struggling with the children to make it without him. Since the copious journals tracked much of her life from 1950 until 1962, fascination with her biography with this important omission only increased.

Ownership of family papers and copyrights have passed down to other generations in the Hughes and Plath families. In some respects, there is still discord over Ted's infidelity to Sylvia that remains a divide in the scholarship (biographies that take one "side" over the other, for example). Serious readers need to remain conscious of source material for what is being written about the poet and stay alert for bias. Cooperation or lack of it by holders of the estate and copyrights, members of the family on either side, occasionally still sets the "camps" of criticism and biography against one another. No matter who claims they knew them firsthand or has a new version of the story to tell, a book that paints Sylvia as a saint and Ted as a devil or vice versa is too simplistic for sophisticated readers of the twenty-first century. A story about human beings and relationships is much more complex, and certainly the relationship between two poets who even worked on the backs of each other's manuscript pages at times has an intriguing dynamic that goes beyond proving who did the most damage to the other.

LEGACY: TWENTIETH-CENTURY AMERICAN POET

As the literary and academic communities begin to look at the twentieth century as a whole and make judgments and assessments about the contributions of its literary practitioners, Sylvia Plath's place as an American poet will be reconsidered among others of her time. Like that of Emily Dickinson, her legacy may benefit from this reconsideration occurring at the same time that more authentic, less heavily edited, editions of her work are appearing—the unabridged journals, for example, published in 2000, and *Ariel*, published in manuscript facsimile with poems in their original number and order published in late 2004. Time will tell if her poems continue to be overshadowed in many circles by the tragedies and mysteries of her biography or if their technical skill, subject matter, and power stand alone through the test of time as the work of a twentieth-century genius. Dickinson's work has survived the mythology of her life; history has yet to see whether Plath's will do the same.

That said, Plath is certainly regarded as an important, if not a generally agreed upon great American poet. Her work explores the intersections of domesticity and art, and digs deep into themes of family relationships and female roles in society. One of the reasons her poetry has endured in anthologies and elsewhere is that it speaks to the female condition. One wonders what turns Plath's work would have made had she lived through the feminist movement of the 1970s and 1980s that came to embrace women's work and life stories so highly. As a dedicated poet who was only 30 years old when she died, her greatest contributions to literature were very likely still ahead of her.

Appendix A

FAMILY TREE

Otto Emil Plath (father)	b. April 13, 1885; d. Nov. 5, 1940.
Aurelia Frances Schober (mother)	b. April 26, 1906; d. Mar. 11, 1994.
Otto and Aurelia Plath	*m. Jan. 4, 1932.*
SYLVIA PLATH	b. Oct. 27, 1932; d. Feb. 11, 1963.
Warren Joseph Plath (brother)	b. April 27, 1935.
Sylvia Plath and Ted Hughes	*m. June 16, 1956.*
Ted Hughes (husband)	b. Aug. 17, 1930; d. Oct. 28, 1998.
Frieda Rebecca Hughes (daughter)	b. Apr. 1, 1960.
Nicholas Farrar Hughes (son)	b. Jan. 17, 1962.

Appendix B

SYLVIA PLATH'S LIBRARY

Below is a selection of Sylvia Plath's reading, based on evidence from her journals, letters, and other writing; surviving books from her library that bear her signature, bookplate, and/or marginalia; school textbooks; and firsthand recollections from people who knew her. Many of the anthologies on the list are course textbooks.

After Many a Summer Dies the Swan, by Aldous Huxley
Alice in Wonderland, by Lewis Carroll
All for Love, by John Dryden
All God's Chillun Got Wings, by Eugene O'Neill
All the King's Men, by Robert Penn Warren
An Anthology of Famous English and American Poetry, edited by Conrad Aiken
Antic Hay: A Novel, by Aldous Huxley
Antigone, by Sophocles
An Armada of Thirty Whales, by Daniel G. Hoffman
The Art of Fiction: An Introduction to Ten Novels and Their Authors, by W. Somerset Maugham
The Art of Teaching, by Gilbert Highet
Babbitt, by Sinclair Lewis
Bacchae, by Euripedes
A Basic History of the United States, by Charles A. Beard and Mary R. Beard
The Battle of the Books, by Jonathan Swift
Best Russian Short Stories, edited by Thomas Seltzer
Der blinde Geronimo und sein Bruder, by Arthur Schnitzler
The Bobbsey Twins series, by Laura Lee Hope et al.

A Book of Dramas, edited by Bruce Carpenter
Book of Mormon, translated by Joseph Smith
Brave New World: A Novel, by Aldous Huxley
Caesar and Cleopatra, by Bernard Shaw
Calling All Girls magazine
Candida, by Bernard Shaw
Cat on a Hot Tin Roof, by Tennessee Williams
Cavalcade of the American Novel: From the Birth of the Nation to the Middle of the Twentieth Century, by Edward Wagenknecht
Cavalcade of the English Novel from Elizabeth to George VI, by Edward Wagenknecht
The Centuries' Poetry: An Anthology, edited by Denys Kilham Roberts
Charles Du Bos and English Literature: A Critic and His Orientation, by Angelo Philip Bertocci
The Charterhouse of Parma, by Stendahl (Marie-Henri Beyle), translated from the French by C. K. Scott Moncrieff
The Chequer'd Shade: Reflections on Obscurity in Poetry, by John Press
The Collected Poems of Edith Sitwell, by Edith Sitwell
The Collected Poems of Dylan Thomas, by Dylan Thomas
The Complete Novels and Selected Tales of Nathaniel Hawthorne, edited by Norman Holmes Pearson
A Comprehensive Anthology of American Poetry, edited by Conrad Aiken
The Courage to Be, by Paul Tillich
Cranford, by Elizabeth Glaskell
Dark of the Moon, by Sara Teasdale
Darkness at Noon, by Arthur Koestler, translated by Daphne Hardy
Darwin, Marx, Wagner: Critique of a Heritage, by Jacques Barzun
Desire under the Elms, by Eugene O'Neill
D. H. Lawrence, Novelist, by F. R. Leaves
The Divine Comedy, by Dante Alighieri
Don Juan in Hell: From Man and Superman, by Bernard Shaw
Drama from Ibsen to Eliot, by Raymond Williams
Duchess of Malfy, by John Webster
Edward the Second, by Christopher Marlowe
Eight Cousins, by Louisa May Alcott
The Eighteenth Century Background: Studies on the Idea of Nature in the Thought of the Period, by Basil Willey
Elements of a Democratic Government, by J. A. Corry
Emilia Galotti, by Gotthold Ephraim Lessing
Eminent British Poets of the Nineteenth Century, edited by Paul Robert Lieder
The Emperor Jones, by Eugene O'Neill
Epstein: An Autobiography, by Sir Jacob Epstein
Escape from Freedom, by Erich Fromm

Essays, edited by Leonard F. Dean
The Experience of Critics, by Christopher Fry
Faust, by Johann Wolfgang von Goethe
Fifty Great Short Stories, edited by Milton Crane
The Flowers of Evil, by Charles Baudelaire
Forty Years of Song, by William Dodge Gray
A Fragment on Government and An Introduction to the Principles of Morals and Legislation, by Jeremy Bentham
Freshman Handbook of 1954, Smith College
The Garden Party, by Katherine Mansfield
Genetrix, by Francois Mauriac
Gone with the Wind, by Margaret Mitchell
A Goodly Heritage, by Mary Ellen Chase
The Grapes of Wrath, by John Steinbeck
Great Companions: Readings on Meanings and Conduct of Life from Ancient and Modern Sources, edited by Robert French Leavens and Mary Agnes Leavens
The Great Gatsby, by F. Scott Fitzgerald
The Great God Brown, by Eugene O'Neill
Growth of the Soil, by Knut Hamsun
Gulliver's Travels, by Jonathan Swift
The Ha-Ha, by Jennifer Dawson
The Hairy Ape, by Eugene O'Neill
Harper's Magazine Reader: A Selection of Articles from Harper's Magazine, 1953
Heartbreak House, by Bernard Shaw
Heaven and Hell, by Aldous Huxley
Heidi, by Johanna Spyri
Hieronymus Bosch: The Garden of Delights, edited by Wolfgang Hirsch
A History of Russian Literature, by D. S. Mirsky
Home Port, by Olive Higgins Prouty
The Horse's Mouth: A Novel, by Joyce Cary
The House of the Dead, by Fyodor Dostoevsky
Howard's End, by E. M. Forster
In Dubious Battle, by John Steinbeck
Introducing Unitarianism: A Dynamic Religion for Life, by John Nicholls Booth
Iphigenie auf Tauris, by Johann Wolfgang von Goethe
Jane Eyre, by Charlotte Brontë
Jean Christophe, by Romain Rolland
Johnny Tremain, by Esther Forbes
Joseph Smith Tells His Own Story, by Joseph Smith
The Lady's Not for Burning: A Comedy, by Christopher Fry
Lazarus Laughed, by Eugene O'Neill

Leaves of Grass, by Walt Whitman

Little Men, by Louisa May Alcott

A Little Treasury of Great Poetry: English & American, from Chaucer to the Present Day, edited by Oscar Williams

Look Homeward, Angel: A Story of the Buried Life, by Thomas Wolfe

The Love Letters of Phyllis McGinley, by Phyllis McGinley

La machine infernale, by Jean Cocteau

Male and Female: A Study of the Sexes in a Changing World, by Margaret Mead

Marco Millions, by Eugene O'Neill

Le marriage de Figaro, by Pierre Augustin Caron de Beaumarchais

Mary Poppins, by P. L. Travers

Mary Poppins Comes Back, by P. L. Travers

The Mayor of Casterbridge, by Thomas Hardy

Mid-Century American Poets, edited by John Ciardi

Mid-Century French Poets, by Wallace Fowlie

Middlemarch, by George Eliot

The Mill on the Floss, by George Eliot

A Milton Handbook, by James Holly Hanford

The Moon in the Yellow River, by Denis Johnston

Mourning Becomes Electra, by Eugene O'Neill

Neighbors: Poems, by Florence Burrill Jacobs

New Outline History of Europe, 1500–1848, by Henry Wilson Littlefield

Nine Plays, by Eugene O'Neill

Nouvelle anthologie francaise, edited by Albert Schinz et. al.

On Liberty, by John Stuart Mill

On Rereading Chaucer, by Howard Rollin Patch

One Hundred Modern Poems, edited by Selden Rodman

An Outline History of the Middle Ages, by George Fox Mott

A Passage to India, by E. M. Forster

Patterns for Living, edited by Oscar James Campbell

Patterns of Culture, by Ruth Benedict

The Penguin Book of Contemporary Verse, edited by Kenneth Allott

Le Pére Goriot, by Honoré de Balzac

The Pocket Book of Robert Frost's Poems, edited by Louis Untermeyer

Poetry and the Age, by Randall Jarrell

Pogo, by Walt Kelly

The Portable James Joyce, by James Joyce

Practical Criticism: A Study of Literary Judgment, by I. A. Richards

Primer for Protestants, by James Hastings Nichols

Pygmalion, by Bernard Shaw

The Revolt of the Masses, by José Ortega y Gasset

Sanctuary, by William Faulkner

The Second Tree from the Corner, by E. B. White

To Secure These Rights: The Report of the President's Committee on Civil Rights, by the U.S. President's Committee on Civil Rights

Selected Writings of Thomas De Quincey, edited by Philip Van Doren Stern

Selections from Chaucer, edited by William Allan Neilson and Howard Rollin Patch

Selections from the Federalist: A Commentary on the Constitution of the United States, edited by Henry Steele Commager

Seven Arts, edited by Fernando Puma

Short Novels of Colette, by Colette

Short Stories: Tradition and Direction, edited by William M. Sale, Jr., James Hall, and Martin Steinmann, Jr.

Short Story Masterpieces, edited by Robert Penn Warren and Albert Erskine

Sister Carrie, by Theodore Dreiser

Spring Birth and Other Poems, by Mark Van Doren

Stories, by Frank O'Connor

Strange Interlude, by Eugene O'Neill

The Strategies and Tactics of World Communism, by the U.S. Congress Committee on Foreign Affairs

A Streetcar Named Desire, by Tennessee Williams

The Sun Also Rises, by Ernest Hemingway

A Tale of a Tub, by Jonathan Swift

Tender Is the Night: A Romance, by F. Scott Fitzgerald

Theatre choisi de Corneille: suivi d'un choix de ses Posies diverses, by Pierre Corneille

Tonio Kroger, by Thomas Mann

Tragedy in Relation to Aristotle's Poetics, by F. L. Lucas

Treasure Island, by Robert Louis Stevenson

The Trumpeter of Krakow, by Eric P. Kelly

Understanding Poetry, by Cleanth Brooks and Robert Penn Warren

The Unicorn: William Butler Yeats's Search for Reality, by Virginia Moore

U.S.A., by John Dos Passos

Vanity Fair: A Novel Without a Hero, by William Makepeace Thackeray

Villette, by Charlotte Brontë

War and Peace, by Leo Tolstoy

The Way of All Flesh, by Samuel Butler

The Wind in the Willows, by Kenneth Grahame

Winnie the Pooh, by A. A. Milne

A Woman Killed with Kindness, by Thomas Heywood

The Yearling, by Marjorie Rawlings Kinnan

BIBLIOGRAPHY

SELECTED WORKS BY SYLVIA PLATH

Plath, Sylvia. *Ariel*. New York: Harper & Row, 1966.

———. *The Bed Book*. New York: Harper & Row, 1976.

———. *The Bell Jar*. New York: Harper & Row, 1971.

———. *The Collected Poems of Sylvia Plath*, ed. Ted Hughes. New York: Harper & Row, 1981.

———. *The Colossus and Other Poems*. New York: Alfred A. Knopf, 1962.

———. *Crossing the Water: Transitional Poems*. New York: Harper & Row, 1971.

———. Interview, *The Poet Speaks*, ed. Peter Orr. New York: Barnes & Noble, 1966, pp. 167–72.

———. *The It-Doesn't-Matter Suit*. New York: St. Martin's Press, 1996.

———. *Johnny Panic and the Bible of Dreams and Other Prose Writings*. London: Faber and Faber, 1977.

———. *The Journals of Sylvia Plath (abridged)*, ed. Frances McCullough. New York: Dial Press, 1982.

———. *Letters Home: Correspondence 1950–1963*, ed. Aurelia Schober Plath. New York: Harper & Row, 1975.

———. *Plath Reads Plath*. Cambridge, MA: Credo Records, 1975.

———. "Review of *The Stones of Troy*." *Gemini* 1, no. 2 (Summer 1957): 98–103.

———. *The Unabridged Journals of Sylvia Plath, 1950–1962*, ed. Karen V. Kukil. New York: Random House, 2000.

———. *Winter Trees*. New York: Harper & Row, 1972.

————, ed. *American Poetry Now: A Selection of the Best Poems by Modern American Writers*. Critical Quarterly Poetry Supplement, 2, 1961.

SECONDARY AND RELATED SOURCES

Aird, Eileen M. *Sylvia Plath: The Woman and Her Work*. New York: Harper & Row, 1973.

Alexander, Paul, ed. *Ariel Ascending: Writings about Sylvia Plath*. New York: Harper & Row, 1984.

————. *Rough Magic: A Biography of Sylvia Plath*. New York: Viking Press, 1991.

Alvarez, A. *The Savage God: A Study of Suicide*. New York: Random House, 1970.

————. "Your Story, My Story." Review of *Birthday Letters*, by Ted Hughes. *The New Yorker*, 2 February 1998, 58–64.

Ames, Lois. "Sylvia Plath: A Biographical Note." In *The Bell Jar*, by Sylvia Plath. New York: Harper & Row, 1971, pp. 277–96. First U.S. edition.

Annas, Pamela J. *A Disturbance in Mirrors: The Poetry of Sylvia Plath*. Westport, CT: Greenwood, 1988.

Axelrod, Steven Gould. *Sylvia Plath: The Wound and the Cure of Words*. Baltimore, MD: Johns Hopkins University Press, 1990.

Barnard, Caroline King. *Sylvia Plath*. Boston: Twayne, 1978.

Bassnet, Susan. *Sylvia Plath*. London: Macmillan Education Ltd., 1987.

Becker, Jillian. *Giving Up: The Last Days of Sylvia Plath: A Memoir*. New York: St. Martin's Press, 2002.

"The Blood Jet Is Poetry." Review of *Ariel*, by Sylvia Plath. *Time* 10 June 1966, 55–56.

Bloom, Harold, ed. *Sylvia Plath*. Modern Critical Views series. New York: Chelsea House Publishers, 1989.

Brain, Tracy. *The Other Sylvia Plath*. Essex, England: Pearson, 2001.

Brennan, Claire. *The Poetry of Sylvia Plath: Essays, Articles, Reviews*. Columbia Critical Guides. New York: Columbia University Press, 1999.

Britzolakis, Christina. *Sylvia Plath and the Theatre of Mourning*. New York: Oxford University Press, 1999.

Broe, Mary Lynn. "A Subtle Psychic Bond: The Mother Figure in Sylvia Plath's Poetry." In *The Lost Tradition: Mothers and Daughters in Literature*, ed. Cathy N. Davidson and E. M. Broner. New York: Ungar, 1980, pp. 217–30.

Brooks, Cleanth, and Robert Penn Warren. *Understanding Poetry: An Anthology for College Students*. New York: Holt, 1938.

Bundtzen, Lynda K. *The Other Ariel*. Amherst: University of Massachusetts Press, 2001.

————. *Plath's Incarnations: Woman and the Creative Process*. Ann Arbor: University of Michigan Press, 1983.

Burroway, Janet. "I Didn't Know Sylvia Plath." *Five Points* 5, no. 3 (Summer 2001): 24–47.

Butscher, Edward, *Sylvia Plath: Method and Madness.* New York: Seabury Press, 1976.

———, ed. *Sylvia Plath: The Woman and the Work.* New York: Dodd, Mead, 1977.

Byatt, A.S. "Sylvia Plath: Letters Home" (1976). In A.S. Byatt, *Passions of the Mind: Selected Writings.* London: Vintage, 1991, pp. 250–54.

Cam, Heather. "'Daddy': Sylvia Plath's Debt to Anne Sexton." *American Literature* 59 (October 1987): 429–32.

Corroll, Rory. "Discovery of Plath's Forgotten Teenage Poems Dismays Friends." *The Guardian,* 20 November 1998, 2.

De Lauretis, Teresa. "Rebirth in *The Bell Jar.*" *Women's Studies* 3 (1975): 173–83.

Dickie, Margaret. *Sylvia Plath and Ted Hughes.* Urbana: University of Illinois Press, 1979.

Ellmann, Mary. "*The Bell Jar:* An American Girlhood." In *The Art of Sylvia Plath: A Symposium,* Charles Newman, ed. London: Faber and Faber, 1970, pp. 221–6.

Faas, Ekbert. "Chapters of a Shared Mythology: Sylvia Plath and Ted Hughes." In *The Achievement of Ted Hughes,* ed. Keith Sagar. Athens: University of Georgia Press, 1983, pp. 107–24.

Gilbert, Sandra M. "A Fine, White Flying Myth: The Life/Work of Sylvia Plath." In *Shakespeare's Sisters: Feminist Essays on Women Poets,* ed. Sandra M. Gilbert and Susan Gubar. Bloomington: Indiana University Press, 1979, pp. 245–60.

———. "In Yeats' House: The Death and Resurrection of Sylvia Plath." In *Critical Essays on Sylvia Plath,* ed. Linda W. Wagner. Boston: G.K. Hall, pp. 204–22.

Hall, Caroline King Barnard. *Sylvia Plath, Revised.* New York: Twayne's United States Author Series (no. 702), 1998.

Hampl, Patricia. "The Smile of Accomplishment: Sylvia Plath's Ambition." *Iowa Review* 25 (1995): 1–28.

Hardwick, Elizabeth. "On Sylvia Plath." In *Ariel Ascending,* ed. Paul Alexander. New York: Harper & Row, 1985, pp. 100–15.

Hargrove, Nancy D. *The Journey Toward Ariel: Sylvia Plath's Poems of 1956–59.* Lund, Sweden: Lund University Press, 1994.

Hayman, Ronald. *The Death and Life of Sylvia Plath.* London: Heinemann, 1991.

Heaney, Seamus. "The Indefatigable Hoof-taps: Sylvia Plath." In *The Government of the Tongue,* ed. Seamus Heaney. London: Faber, 1988, pp. 148–70.

Helle, Anita. "'Family Matters': An Afterword on the Biography of Sylvia Plath," *Northwest Review,* 26, no. 2 (1988): 148–60.

Holbrook, David. *Sylvia Plath: Poetry and Existence*. London: Athlone, 1976.

Hughes, Ted. *Birthday Letters*. New York: Farrar, Straus & Giroux, 1998.

——. Foreword to *The Journals of Sylvia Plath, 1950–62*, ed. Frances McCullough. New York: Dial Press, 1982.

——. Introduction to *The Collected Poems of Sylvia Plath*, ed. Ted Hughes. New York: Harper & Row, 1981.

——. Introduction to *"Johnny Panic and the Bible of Dreams and Other Prose Writings,"* by Sylvia Plath. London: Faber and Faber, 1977.

——. "Publishing Sylvia Plath" (1971). In *Winter Pollen: Occasional Prose*, ed. William Scammell. London: Faber, 1995, pp. 163–69.

——. "Sylvia Plath and Her Journals" (1982). In *Winter Pollen: Occasional Prose*, ed. William Scammell. London: Faber, 1995, pp. 177–90.

——. "Sylvia Plath and The Evolution of 'Sheep in Fog'" (1988). In *Winter Pollen: Occasional Prose*, ed. William Scammell. London: Faber, 1995, pp. 191–211.

——. "Sylvia Plath's *Crossing the Water*: Some Reflections." *Critical Quarterly* 13 (Summer 1971): 165–72.

Kakutani, Michiko. "A Portrait of Plath in Poetry for Its Own Sake." *New York Times*, 13 February 1998, B43.

Kamel, Rose. " 'A Self to Recover': Sylvia Plath's Bee Cycle Poems." *Modern Poetry Series* 47 (1977): 74–85.

Kendall, Tim. *Sylvia Plath: A Critical Study*. London: Faber and Faber, 2001.

Kirkham, Michael. "Sylvia Plath." In *Sylvia Plath: The Critical Heritage*, ed. Linda W. Wagner. London: Routledge, 1988, pp. 276–91.

Klein, Elinor. "A Friend Recalls Sylvia Plath." *Glamour* (November 1966): 168, 184.

Kroll, Jack. "Answering Ariel." Review of *Birthday Letters*, by Ted Hughes. *Newsweek*, 2 February 1998, 58–59.

Kroll, Judith. *Chapters in a Mythology. The Poetry of Sylvia Plath*. New York: Harper & Row, 1976.

Kukil, Karen V. "True to Her Words." *Smith Alumni Quarterly Online*, Spring 2001. http://backissues.saqonline.smith.edu/aarticle.epl?articleid = 168 (accessed March 5, 2004).

Lane, Gary, ed. *Sylvia Plath: New Views on the Poetry*. Baltimore, MD: Johns Hopkins University Press, 1979.

Lowell, Robert. "Foreword" to *Ariel*. In *Ariel*, by Sylvia Plath. London: Faber and Faber, 1965, pp. ix–xi. First English edition.

Macpherson, Pat. *Reflecting on "The Bell Jar."* London: Routledge, 1991.

Malcolm, Janet. *The Silent Woman: Sylvia Plath and Ted Hughes*. New York: Knopf, 1994.

Markey, Janice. *A Journey into the Red Eye: The Poetry of Sylvia Plath—A Critique*. London: The Women's Press, 1993.

Marsack, Robyn. *Sylvia Plath*. Buckingham, England: Open University Press, 1992.

McClatchy, J. D. "Short Circuits and Folding Mirrors" (1979). In *Sylvia Plath*, ed. Harold Bloom. New York: Chelsea House Publishers, 1989, pp. 79–93.

McCullough, Frances. "Foreword to the Twenty-Fifth Anniversary Edition." In *The Bell Jar*, by Sylvia Plath. Twenty-Fifth Anniversary hardcover edition. New York: HarperCollins, 1996, pp. ix–xviii.

Middlebrook, Diane Wood. *Everyman's Library Pocket Poets: Sylvia Plath*. New York: Alfred A. Knopf, 1998.

———. *Her Husband: Hughes and Plath—A Marriage*. New York: Viking, 2003.

Newman, Charles, ed. *The Art of Sylvia Plath*. Bloomington: Indiana University Press, 1970.

Oates, Joyce Carol. "The Death Throes of Romanticism: The Poetry of Sylvia Plath." In *New Heaven, New Earth: The Visionary Experience in Literature*. London: Victor Gollancz, 1976, pp. 111–40.

Orr, Peter. *The Poet Speaks*. London: Routledge, 1966.

Ostriker, Alicia. "The Americanization of Sylvia." In *Critical Essays on Sylvia Plath*, ed. Linda W. Wagner. Boston: G. K. Hall, 1984, pp. 97–109.

———. *Stealing the Language: The Emergence of Women's Poetry in America*. London: The Women's Press, 1986.

Pearson, Allison. "Trapped in Time: Sylvia Plath." *The Daily Telegraph*. 1 April 2000, Arts & Books Section, A1–A2.

Pereira, Malin Walther. "Be(e)ing and 'Truth': *Tar Baby's* Signifying on Sylvia Plath's Bee Poems." *Twentieth Century Literature* 42, no. 4 (Winter 1996): 526–34.

Perloff, Marjorie G. "Extremist Poetry: Some Versions of the Sylvia Plath Myth." *Journal of Modern Literature* 2 (November 1972): 581–88.

———. "Sylvia Plath's 'Sivvy' Poems: A Portrait of the Poet as Daughter." In *Sylvia Plath: New Views on the Poetry*, ed. Gary Lane. Baltimore, MD: Johns Hopkins University Press, 1979, pp. 155–77.

———. "The Two Ariels: The (Re)Making of the Sylvia Plath Canon." In *Poems in Their Place: The Intertexuality and Order of Poetic Collections*, ed. Neil Fraistat. Chapel Hill: University of North Carolina Press, 1986, pp. 308–33.

Plath, Otto Emil. *Bumblebees and Their Ways*. New York: Macmillan, 1934.

Rorem, Ned. *Ariel: Five Poems of Sylvia Plath, for Soprano, Clarinet and Piano*. (musical score). New York: Boosey & Hawkes, 1974.

Rose, Jacqueline. *The Haunting of Sylvia Plath*. Cambridge, MA: Harvard University Press, 1991.

———. "So Many Lives, So Little Time." *The Observer*. 2 April 2000, Review Section, 11.

Rosenblatt, Jon. *Sylvia Plath: The Poetry of Initiation*. Chapel Hill: University of North Carolina Press, 1979.

Rosenthal, M.L. "Sylvia Plath and the Confessional Poetry" (1967). In *The Art of Sylvia Plath*, ed. Charles Newman. Bloomington: Indiana University Press, 1970, pp. 69–76.

Rowley, Rosemarie. "Electro-Convulsive Treatment in Sylvia Plath's Life and Work." *Thumbscrew* 10 (Spring 1998): 87–99.

Sambrook, Hana. *York Notes: Sylvia Plath: Selected Works*. Harlow, England: Longman York Press, 1990.

Sheldon, Michael. "The 'Demon' that Killed Sylvia." *The Daily Telegraph*, 13 March 2000, 9.

Steiner, George. "'Dying Is an Art.'" In *The Art of Sylvia Plath: A Symposium*, ed. Charles Newman. London: Faber and Faber, 1970, pp. 211–18.

Steiner, Nancy Hunter. *A Closer Look at Ariel: A Memory of Sylvia Plath*. London: Faber, 1974.

Stevenson, Anne. *Bitter Fame: A Life of Sylvia Plath*. Boston: Houghton Mifflin, 1989.

———. "Sylvia Plath's Word Games." *Poetry Review* 86, no. 4 (Winter 1996/7): 28–34.

Timmerman, John H. "Plath's Mirror." *Explicator* 45 (1987): 63–64.

Van Dyne, Susan R., "'More Terrible Than She Ever Was': The Manuscripts of Sylvia Plath's Bee Poems." In *Stings: Original Drafts of the Poem in Facsimile Reproduced from the Sylvia Plath Collection at Smith College*, by Sylvia Plath. Northampton, MA: Smith College Library Mortimer Rare Book Room, 1982, pp. 3–12.

———. *Revising Life: Sylvia Plath's "Ariel" Poems*. Chapel Hill: University of North Carolina Press, 1993.

Wagner, Erica. *Ariel's Gift: Ted Hughes, Sylvia Plath and the Story of "Birthday Letters"*. London: Faber and Faber, 2000.

———. "At Last, Justice for Hughes." *The Times*, 10 April 2000, 6–7.

———. "Love That Passed All Understanding." *The Times*, 18 March 2000, 21.

Wagner-Martin, Linda, ed. *Critical Essays on Sylvia Plath*. Boston: G.K. Hall and Co., 1984.

———. *Sylvia Plath: A Biography*. New York: St. Martin's Press, 1987.

———. *Sylvia Plath: The Critical Heritage*. New York: Routledge, 1988.

REFERENCES

Meyering, Sheryl. *Sylvia Plath: A Reference Guide, 1973–1988*. Boston: G.K. Hall, 1990.

Tabor, Stephen. *Sylvia Plath: An Analytical Bibliography*. London: Mansell, 1987.

AUDIO/VISUAL MATERIALS

Plath, Sylvia. *Plath Reads Plath*. Cambridge, MA: Credo Records, 1975.

Voices and Visions: Sylvia Plath. The New York Center for Visual History, Inc., VHS. 1988.

WEB SITES

Academy of American Poets. "Sylvia Plath." http://www.poets.org/poets/poets. cfm?45442B7C000C0704 (accessed 29 September 2004).

INDEX

Abels, Cyrilly, 41, 45, 48, 62
The Admirable Crichton (Barrie), 33
"Admonitions," 59
"Adolescence," 32
"After great pain, a formal feeling comes—" (Dickinson), 3
Agamemnon (Aeschylus), 33
Alice J. Phillips Junior School, 25
"Alone and Alive," 31
Alvarez, A., 84, 91, 99
Amherst College, 36
"Amnesiac," 97
"Among the Narcissi," 90
"And Summer Will Not Come Again," 34, 38
Annie F. Warren Grammar School, 18
"April Aubade," 64
"Ariel," 95
Ariel and Other Poems, 2, 3, 28, 94–96, 109
"Ariel's Song," 28–29, 95
Arrowsmith (Lewis), 33
Art, 5, 31, 47, 58

"A Secret," 94
The Atlantic Monthly, 32, 64, 65, 97
Auden, W. H., 44
"A Winter's Tale," 82
"A Wish upon a Star," 26
"A Youth's Plea for World Peace," 34
Azalea Path, 22, 81

"Balloons," 100
Barnhouse, Ruth Tiffany, Dr., 56–57, 80, 81, 94
"Barren Women," 85
Bartz, Lydia Clara, 10
Bartz, Rupert, 10
"Battle-Scene," 78
BBC (British Broadcasting Corporation), 3, 5, 84, 87, 96
"Beach Plum Season on Cape Cod," 79
Becker, Jillian and Gerry, 100–102
The Bed Book, 81
Beekeeping, 91
Bees, 11, 13, 91, 94

The Bell Jar, 7, 17, 35, 39, 45, 88, 91, 92, 95, 99, 100, 108
The Belmont Hotel, 40–41
Benét, Stephen Vincent, 37
Birthday Letters (Hughes), 73
"Bitter Strawberries," 36
"Blackberrying," 87
"Black Rook in Rainy Weather," 77, 79
Blackwell, Elizabeth (Betsy) Talbot, 47, 50, 51
The Bobbsey Twins, 28
The Boston Globe, 55, 56
The Boston Herald, 34
Boston, Massachusetts, 11–12, 18, 23, 28, 79–82
Boston University, 9, 11, 24, 80
Bowen, Elizabeth, 44, 51
The Bradford, 31, 32
Bradford High School, Gamaliel, 30–34, 80
Broadsheet, 70
Brookline High School, 11
Brown, Marcia, 42
Buckley, Maureen, 39
Buddenbrooks (Mann), 33
Bumblebees and Their Ways (Plath, Otto), 13–15, 21
"By Candlelight," 95

The Calm (Hughes), 95
Cambridge, England, 68–77
Cambridge University, 65, 67–77
"Candles," 84
Cantor, Margaret, family, 41, 43
Cape Cod, Massachusetts, 54, 59, 77
"Carnival Nocturne," 43
Catcher in the Rye (Salinger), 39
Chequer, 71
"Child," 100

The Christian Science Monitor, 34, 36, 42, 64, 76, 79
"Circus in Three Rings," 62, 65
"City Streets," 32
Cohen, Eddie, 38
The Collected Poems, 109
The Colossus and Other Poems, 82, 83, 85, 88, 98
Court Green, 86–88, 89–90, 91, 94
Crocketteers, 32
Crockett, Wilbury, 30–34, 41, 52, 106
"Crossing the Water," 90
"Cut," 95

"Daddy," 20, 95, 97
"Danse macabre," 64
David Copperfield (Dickens), 29
Davis, Bette, 27, 37
Davison, Peter, 62, 67
Death Comes for the Archbishop (Cather), 33
"Den of Lions," 38
"Denouement," 59
Depression, 4, 39
Devon, England, 86–88, 98
"Dialogue over a Ouija Board," 77
Diaries, childhood, 26–29
Dickinson, Emily, 1, 2, 3, 8, 28, 106, 110
Doctor Faustus (Mann), 33
"Doom of Exiles," 58
"Doomsday," 43, 59
Dostoevsky, Fyodor, 61, 63
Double Exposure, 98

"East Wind," 32
"Edge," 100
Edman, Irwin, 32
Electroshock therapy, 53–54, 57
Eliot, T. S., 81, 84

"Elm," 90
Emerson, Ralph Waldo, 33
Emory University, 2
"Epitaph," 64
Ethan Frome (Wharton), 33
"Event," 91

"Face Lift," 85
Fall Creek, Wisconsin, 10
Feminist movement, 1
"First Appearance," 90
"For a Fatherless Son," 94
Ford, Art, 48
"The Forsaken Merman"
    (Arnold), 18
"Four Young Poets," 80
Freeman, Ruth, 67
Fulbright, 41, 65, 70
"Full Fathom Five," 83

German: heritage, 7, 9; language,
    5, 9, 11; pen pal, 29
"Gigolo," 100
Girl Scouts, 4, 25, 26, 31
"Go Get the Goodly Squab," 43,
    62
"Gone Is the River," 32
Gone with the Wind (Mitchell), 26,
    117
"The Great Gildersleeve," 27
Greenwood (also Grunwald),
    Aurelia, 8
Greenwood (also Grunwald),
    Joseph, 7
Guest-editorship, 45–51

Harper's, 43, 59, 62
Harvard University, 10, 44, 49, 52,
    59
Haskell, Joseph, 11
Haven House, 36, 39, 40

The Hawk in the Rain (Hughes),
    76, 78
"Heavy Women," 85
Heidi (Spyri), 15, 117
Hiroshima, Japan, 29
Hughes, Frieda Rebecca, birth, 83,
    85, 86
Hughes, Nicholas Farrar, 89
Hughes, Olwyn, 86, 91
Hughes, Ted, 1–2, 3; editing
    Sylvia's work, 108–10; marriage,
    74; meeting Sylvia, 70–72
Hunter, Nancy, 59–61
Hurricane of 1938, Great New
    England, 18–19
Hypnosis, 82, 83

"I Lied for Love," 44
"I'll tell you how the sun rose"
    (Dickinson), 28
"Initiation," 42
"Insect Societies" (Plath, Otto), 15
"In the Corner of My Garden," 26
"In the Mountains," 62
Ireland, 93–94
Italy, 69
"I Thought That I Could Not Be
    Hurt," 31

"The Jack Benny Show," 25, 27
Jane Eyre (Brontë), 25, 117; film,
    25
"Johnny Panic and the Bible of
    Dreams," 80
Journals, 37, 40, 106–7
The Journals of Sylvia Plath, 109
Joyce, James, 52, 74
Judy Bolton series, 28

Kazin, Alfred, 61–62, 85
"Kindness," 100

Kinsella, Thomas, 93
Kirsten Lavransdatter (Undset), 33

Ladies' Home Journal, 32, 80
"Lady Lazarus," 96
"Lament," 64
Lameyer, Gordon, 59, 61, 63, 67, 70
Lassie Come Home, 25
"Law in the Country of the Cats" (Hughes), 71
Lawrence House, 36, 42, 58, 59
"Leaving Early," 84
Legacy, 110–11
Letters Home, 32
LeVarn, Carol, 48
Lewis, Sinclair, 37
Life Poem Book, 26
"Little Fugue," 90
London, England, 7, 86, 88, 96; winter of 1962–1963, 96–99
"Lonely Song," 32
"The Lone Ranger," 25
"Love Is a Parallax," 64
Lowell, Robert, 3, 80, 85
Lucas, Victoria, 35, 88, 99
Lupercal (Hughes), 83, 84
"Lyonnesse," 95

Macdonald, Margot, 34
Mademoiselle, 27, 39, 40, 41, 44, 58, 63, 65, 78, 80; guest-editorship, 45–51
"Mad Girl's Love Song," 51
The Magic Mirror: A Study of the Double in Two of Dostoevsky's Novels, 63
Main Street (Lewis), 33
"Man in Black," 81
Marilyn Monroe, 5

Marshall Perrin Elementary School, 25
"Mary's Song," 97
"The Matisse Chapel," 69–70
Mayo, Frederick, 38
McCarthy, Joseph, 47
McLean Hospital, 57
"Medusa," 95
Meet My Folks! (Hughes), 81
Mental illness, 4
Millay, Edna St. Vincent, 37
"Mirror," 87
"*Mlle's* Last Word," 48, 51
Moore, Marianne, 64
"Morning Song," 85
Mount Holyoke College, 36, 63
Murchison, Carl, 15
Music, 5, 26, 31
"Mussel Hunter at Rock Harbor," 79
My Antonia (Cather), 33
"My Mother and I," 19
"Mystic," 100

Nazis, 29, 95
"Never to Know More Than You Should," 59
Newnham College, Cambridge, 69
The New Yorker, 43, 48, 63, 70, 77, 79, 81, 82, 84, 85, 97
New York Harbor, 10
New York, New York, 27, 44, 45–51, 67, 77
"Nick and the Candlestick," 96
"Nocturne," 79
Norris, Myra Nurse, 103–4
Northampton, Massachusetts, 36, 37
Northwestern College, 10
Norton, Dick, 39, 42, 59

Norton, Mildred, 25
Norton, Perry, 34
"November Graveyard," 78
Now, Voyager (Prouty), 37

"Ocean 1212-W," 98
O'Connor, Frank, 44, 52, 59, 92
"Ode to a Bitten Plum," 37
"On Deck," 84
"On the Decline of Oracles," 78
Ouija board, 76, 93
Oliver Twist (Dickens), 29

Paper dolls, 27
Paradise Pond, 36, 37, 79, 80
"Parallax," 62
"Paralytic," 100
Paris, France, 7, 69
"Parliament Hill Fields," 85
"The Perfect Setup," 40, 42
"Perils of Dew," 19
"Perseus," 78
"Pheasant," 90
The Phillipian, 26
Plath, Aurelia Frances Schober
    (mother), 7–9, 11–16, 19–25,
    42, 75, 77, 86; at Court Green,
    91–93, 95, 97
Plath, Otto Emil (father), 9–11,
    11–16, 19–25, 75, 107; death,
    22; Sylvia visiting his grave, 81
Plath, Sylvia: birth, 12; death,
    103–4; high school, 30–34;
    junior high school, 25–30;
    name, 12; marriage, 74
Plath, Warren Joseph (brother),
    15, 16, 22, 25, 49, 55, 73, 87,
    95
"Poem," 23
"Poem for a Birthday," 82, 85

"The Poet and the Poetess"
    (Alvarez, essay), 84
"Poets on Campus," 48, 51
Point Counter Point (Huxley), 33
"Point Shirley," 81
Point Shirley, Massachusetts, 8,
    15, 20, 38
"Poppies in October," 95
Popular culture, 27
Powley, Betsy, 25, 28
Pride and Prejudice (Austen), 29
Prospero, 28
Prouty, Olive Higgins, 37, 38, 45,
    56, 68, 74, 94, 97
"Purdah," 96

Queen Elizabeth II, 54, 69
"Question," 32

Rape, alleged, 60
Republic (Plato), 33
Return of the Native (Hardy), 33
"Rewards of a New England
    Summer," 36
Roethke, Theodore, 85
Roosevelt, Franklin D., 27
Rosenberg, Julius and Ethel, 47, 50

Sassoon, Richard, 62, 63, 70, 73
Saxton Grant, Eugene F., 85, 88
The Scarlet Pimpernel (Emmuska),
    29
Schober, Aurelia (grandmother),
    7, 31, 52, 54, 55, 67, 70
Schober, Dorothy, "Aunt Dot"
    (aunt), 8, 25, 98, 104
Schober, Frank (also Franz)
    (grandfather), 7, 54, 67
Schober, Frank (uncle), 8
"Second Winter," 65, 80

Sesame and Lilies (Ruskin), 33

Seventeen, 32, 37, 38, 39, 40, 42, 43

Sewanee Review, 82

Sexton, Anne, 4, 80, 81

Shakespeare, William, 28, 68, 95

Shakin, Carl, 68

"Sheep in Fog," 100

A Shropshire Lad (Housman), 33

Sinusitis, 39, 41

"Sketchbook of a Spanish Summer," 76

"Sleep in the Mohave Desert," 84

Smith College, 5, 17, 30, 32, 35–45, 58–65, 67, 85; teaching, 78–79

The Smith Review, 40, 44, 58, 65

"Snake-charmer," 78

"Snow," 19

Snow White, 27

"Sonnet: To a Dissembling Spring," 43

Spain, 75

"Spinster," 77, 79

Sports, 31

St. Botolph's Review, 71

"Stings," 14, 94

"Stopping Dead," 95

Sub-Debs Sorority, 31

Suicide, 99–104; attempt 34, 51–58

"Sunday at the Mintons," 40, 41, 44

Sunshine School, 17–18

"Superman and Paula Brown's New Snowsuit," 65

A Tale of Two Cities (Dickens), 29

Tales From Shakespeare (Lamb), 15, 28

The Tempest (Shakespeare), 15, 28, 95

"The Applicant," 94

"The Arrival of the Bee Box," 14, 94, 97

"The Beekeeper's Daughter," 14

"The Bee Meeting," 14, 94

"The Colossus," 20, 82

"The Courage of Shutting-up," 94

"The Daughters of Blossom Street," 84

"The Day Mr. Prescott Died," 76

"The Dead," 58

"The Departure of the Ghost," 78

"The Detective," 94

"The Disquieting Muses," 78

"The Dream," 78

"The Farewell," 32

"The Fearful," 97

"The Fifty-ninth Bear," 82

"The Ghost's Leavetaking," 78, 79

"The Invalid," 32

"The Jailer," 95

"The Laundromat Affair," 77

"The Manor Garden," 82

"The Moon and the Yew Tree," 87

"The Munich Mannequins," 100

"The Netmenders," 84

"The Rabbit Catcher," 91

"The Sleepers," 83

"The Stones," 82–83

"The Swarm," 14, 94

"The Thought-Fox" (Hughes), 77

"The Thrilling Journey of a Penny," 26

"The Trouble-making Mother," 77

"This Earth Our Hospital," 82

Thomas, Dylan, 48, 50, 62, 74

Thomas, Trevor, 100, 104

"Thoughts," 19

" 'Three Caryatids without a Portico' by Hugo Robus: A Study in Cultural Dimensions," 70

"To Eva Descending the Stair," 43

Tolkien, J. R. R., 15

"Totem," 100

True Story, 44

"Tulips," 85

"Twelfth Night," 43

Twenty Thousand Leagues Under the Sea (Verne), 29

"Two Campers in Cloud Country," 84

"Two Lovers and a Beachcomber by the Real Sea," 64, 65

The Unabridged Journals of Sylvia Plath, 2

Understanding Poetry (Brooks and Warren), 3, 30

United Nations, 46, 49

University of Washington, 10

"Verbal Calisthenics," 59, 64

"Virgin in a Tree," 78

Vogue, 63, 64

Wagner, Janet, 50

War and Peace (Tolstoy), 58

Washington, D. C., 67

The Waste Land (Eliot), 33

"Watercolor of Grantchester Meadows," 81, 84

Wellesley College, 24, 32

Wellesley, Massachusetts, 24, 29, 32, 39, 41, 49, 52

Wevill, Assia, 87, 90, 92, 101, 106–7

Wevill, David, 87, 90

"White Phlox," 32, 42

"Whitsun," 85

Wind in the Willows (Grahame), 15

Winesburg, Ohio (Anderson), 33

Winnie the Pooh (Milne), 15

"Wintering," 94, 97

"Winter Trees," 97

"Winter Words," 64

Winthrop, Massachusetts, 9, 15, 17–25, 39

Woolf, Virginia, 37

"Words," 100

"Words Heard, by Accident, over the Phone," 92

World War II, 1, 27

"Wuthering Heights," 87

Yaddo Writers' Colony, 82–83

"Years," 97

Yeats, William Butler, 93, 96

"Youth's Appeal for Peace," 31

"Zoo Keeper's Wife," 85

About the Author

CONNIE ANN KIRK is an independent scholar whose primary research interests include America literature and poetry and children's literature. She is a Mark Twain Quarry Farm Research Fellow and an Ezra Jack Keats/de Grummond Collection Children's Literature Research Fellow. She is a frequent contributor to Greenwood's Biography series. She is the author of *J. K. Rowling: A Biography* (2003), *Mark Twain: A Biography* (2004), and *Emily Dickinson: A Biography* (2004). She is currently working on the *Companion to American Children's Picture Books* and a *Thematic Guide to Children's Literature* (both forthcoming from Greenwood). Her other forthcoming books include *A Student's Guide to Robert Frost* and *Emily Dickinson and Children*. For further information about the author, visit her Web site: www.connieannkirk.com.